London

Gibraltar

Malta   Cyprus

Alexandria

Cairo   Suez Canal

EGYPT (BR. PROT.)

Delhi

Karachi

Calcutta

ANGLO-EGYPTIAN SUDAN

Aden

INDIA   **BURMA**   **Hong Kong**

NIGERIA

Lagos

Sokotra

Bombay

Madras

Trincomalee

BRITISH NORTH BORNEO

GOLD COAST

BRITISH SOMALILAND

UGANDA

KENYA

Colombo

CEYLON

Penang Malacca

MALAYA

Labuan

Brunei

NEW GUINEA

Solomon Is.

Singapore

SARAWAK

Seychelles

nsion

RHODESIA

Zanzibar

Cocos Is.

AUSTRALIA

CHUANALAND

elena

Mauritius

Brisbane

Walvis Bay →

üderitz Bay →

SWAZILAND

BASUTOLAND

Perth

Adelaide

Norfolk I.

Sydney

Melbourne

Cunha

Cape of Good Hope

SOUTH AFRICA

TASMANIA

Hobart

t its greatest extent

THE BRITISH EMPIRE

THE
BRITISH

CANADA

CAPE OF GOOD HOPE

STRAITS SETTLEMENTS.

1837

COLIN CROSS

EMPIRE

NEW ZEALAND

NEW SOUTH WALES

VICTORIA

1897

LONDON · NEW YORK
SYDNEY · TORONTO

LYN

*The George V Durbar of 1911.
George took the title Emperor of
India extremely seriously, and
insisted on inaugurating his reign
in person, the only British
monarch ever to have done so.
At the old capital of Delhi he
reviewed an enormous parade of
troops and received the homage
of Indian princes.*

Published by
The Hamlyn Publishing Group Ltd
London · New York · Sydney · Toronto
Hamlyn House
Feltham, Middlesex, England

© Copyright The Hamlyn Publishing Group Ltd 1972

ISBN 0 600 31205 4

Printed in Spain by
Mateu Cromo Artes Graficas S.A.,
Madrid

Contents

The British in India. A tennis
party at the end of the
nineteenth century.

How do you like our rule?

The British Empire was a relatively short-lived institution. It lasted for at the most three centuries and was at its peak for only about half a century. Yet in terms of sheer physical extent it was the biggest empire that has ever existed. At one time it covered a quarter of the world and was established in every continent.

In the early twentieth century, some people saw it as a potential world government. Two American professors, writing in 1918, described the intimate consultations between Britain and the leaders of the self-governing dominions as the model on which a future world family of nations should be based. Cecil Rhodes, the cranky financial genius who seized 450,000 square miles of Africa and named them after himself, adopted a complete 'master-race' concept: the British, with some assistance from the Americans and the Germans, were destined to dominate the whole globe.

Yet within half a century of Rhodes's death in 1906, the British Empire was approaching its end. Partly because the British were too liberal by nature to rule tyrannically, and partly because world circumstances had changed, it became clear that the empire had been even more temporary than most political systems.

Yet in spite of its transient nature, the British Empire had some lasting influence. For example, the United States of America, the most powerful country of the twentieth century, was originally a group of British colonies and British influences upon it have always been of great importance. The United States uses the English language, its legal system is based upon the English common law and its constitution is founded largely on what the British constitution was thought to be in the eighteenth century, with the difference that an elected president replaced the hereditary monarch. Nearly all presidents of the United States—the exceptions are Hoover, Roosevelt and Eisenhower—have borne distinctively British names. The great nineteenth-century German chancellor, Otto von Bismarck, thought that it was the most important fact of his day 'that North America speaks English'. However, the United States had become independent long before the British Empire had reached its maturity, and perhaps the most enduring legacy of the British Empire was its role in the creation of a single world.

Until the sixteenth century, the world consisted of several independent cultures which existed in isolation from one another. Europe and China knew practically nothing of each other and neither knew anything of the Inca or Aztec civilisations in America. For an Englishman to visit Russia or India was the equivalent of a modern trip to the moon. In the twentieth century, in contrast, the various world cultures are in continual contact and constantly influencing one another: a civil war in such a country as Vietnam is capable of attracting world-wide attention. The British Empire, which briefly bound a quarter of the world into a single unit, was the leading agent by which the ideas of Europe, at their most vigorous, were transmitted to the rest of the world.

No single ruler or soldier created the British Empire. There was no British Napoleon or Genghis Khan. Indeed a good deal of the empire was acquired without Britain particularly seeking or even wanting it. When Uganda joined the empire in 1891, *Punch* ran a wry cartoon showing John Bull looking at a black baby on his doorstep and saying: 'What, another? Well, I suppose I must take it in!' In the days of the British conquest of India, when it took a year for a letter to reach London and the reply to come back, every move was dictated by the ambitions and necessities of the men on the spot. The British Empire was built up by a series of individuals who snatched at a good chance when they saw it, individuals such as the pirate, Francis Drake, who laid the foundations of British sea power, Clive and Hastings, who built up British dominion in India, Raffles, who

Above: *children gaze at the statue of Queen Victoria in Colombo, Ceylon. Ceylon, originally a Dutch possession, was made a crown colony in 1798, and in the nineteenth century was modernised by the British, who opened schools and a university.*
Below: *a carving from Sierra Leone, thought to represent Queen Victoria, 'the Great White Queen'.*

founded Singapore, Cook and Vancouver, who broke new ground in exploration, Lugard, who established British power in Uganda and Nigeria, and James Brooke, who carved out a hereditary kingdom for himself as rajah of Sarawak.

Very few of the most prominent people in Britain itself took much interest in the empire. Most of the monarchs until George V regarded it as a matter of subsidiary significance. The most famous military commanders, Marlborough and Wellington on land and Nelson at sea, won their reputations in European wars. Of the politicians of the top rank, only Disraeli, Joseph Chamberlain and Winston Churchill took more than a passing interest, and even their careers were dominated by domestic and European considerations.

By the early twentieth century, however, in one way or another, the British quarter of the world had come into existence. It consisted of about fifty different territories, most of which are now independent states. To list them all would be tedious but they can be divided into various categories.

The most significant was India, an empire in itself. What used to be British India is now three separate republics – India, Pakistan and Burma. In terms of population, British India was the second biggest country in the world after China and it lay completely under British domination. It made such a huge centre of gravity as to influence the whole of British policy elsewhere. Such territories as the western, southern and eastern African colonies, Egypt, the Mediterranean colonies, Aden and the Persian Gulf and Malaya had been acquired at least in part on the pretext of guarding the route between Britain and India.

The next major category is the dominions of white settlement – Canada, Australia and New Zealand, which early acquired their own internal self-government but were proud to be associated with the British Empire for external purposes. Such was the fruitfulness and energy of the British nation that it provided not only the biggest source of immigrants to the United States, but also, almost as a sideline, populated these other new countries.

A miscellany of smaller territories, ranging from the British West Indies to about a hundred Pacific islands, which had been collected for various reasons at various times, completes the picture. No single person could know the whole British Empire, indeed it was so diverse that it is difficult to generalise about it. On the whole, however, it can be stated that the British crown and government were supreme everywhere within it, that all education and administration was in the English language and that imperial administration provided a career for many thousands of British men.

The consciousness that Britain had an empire did not arise until the late nineteenth century. In 1877 Queen Victoria, on the proposal of Disraeli, assumed the title of Empress of India. Then, as a result of the work of pioneer explorers came the 'scramble for Africa' in which the European powers partitioned the continent. Britain got the lion's share. Queen Victoria's jubilees in 1887 and 1897, with processions including representatives of diverse overseas territories, dramatised the world power Britain had acquired. People began theorising about it and proclaiming a British world 'destiny'. The Edwardian song *Land of Hope and Glory*, with its vaunting aspiration ('Wider still and wider shall thy bounds be set') belonged to this period, as did the poetry of Rudyard Kipling. Even people who had never in their lives left Britain, and never intended to do so, became proud that their fellow countrymen ruled over multitudes of alien races. There was the story of a London bootblack who looked up at an Indian rajah whose boots he was cleaning and said patronisingly, 'How do you like our rule?'

The process of imperial expansion continued into the twentieth century, and during the First World War the British ac-

quired significant new territories, including Palestine, Iraq and Tanganyika. Between the two world wars, colonial administration was rationalised and a series of quasi-theological definitions associated with the Statute of Westminster set out the contradiction that the self-governing dominions were simultaneously independent and members of 'the British Commonwealth of Nations'. In fact the unanimous and voluntary agreement of the dominions to fight in the First World War had been the result of sentiment rather than of any constitutional arrangement. Torrents of books, some by respected historians, poured off the presses to show that the British Empire was beneficent and could be permanent. 'Empire Day' was celebrated with schoolchildren lining up before the union flag to sing patriotic songs and to listen to imperialistic speeches. As late as 1945 an Oxford don, Lord Elton, published his best-selling 'Imperial Commonwealth' and ended by speculating on 'what wider destiny awaits to be unrolled'.

Thus, although the British Empire was transient it did, for at least half a century, seem to be a permanent, normal institution. It set its mark upon both Britain and the world.

Left: *the memorial in Cape Town to Cecil Rhodes, empire builder extraordinary, who seized 450,000 square miles of Africa and named them after himself.*

Below left: *a gentleman with his pipe bearer, about 1813.*

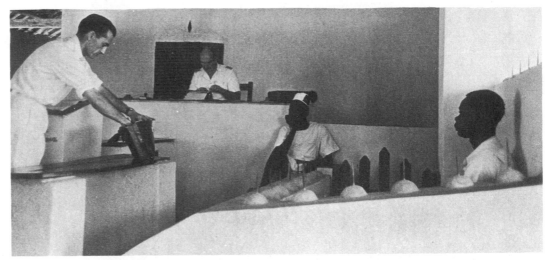

Many *British systems, such as those of justice and education, still prevail in the countries that were once colonies.*
Above: *a British official in the Sudan.*
Right: *a school in Kenya with a picture of Queen Elizabeth II, in full regalia, on the wall.*

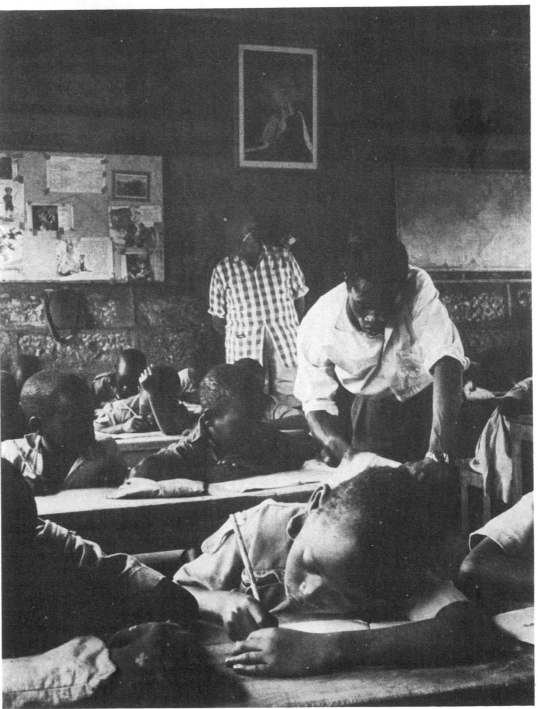

Nova Albion

Henry Hudson's first voyage in search of new trade and a route to China by way of the Arctic regions was made in 1607 for the Muscovy Company. On a subsequent voyage, for the Dutch East India Company, he entered the bay of New York and sailed up the river which is now named after him.

Most of the great empires of history have come about through expansion and conquest over a continuous mass of land. The British Empire, the greatest of them all, grew up, in contrast, largely through sea power, with its component parts widely separated. There is never likely to be a similar empire in the future: the super-powers of the mid-twentieth century rely primarily upon the air, and are even exploring the uses of outer space. The British, however, were superlative seamen who built up their supremacy with the use of ships.

For most of the history of mankind there were few ocean-going ships. Although the Vikings did cross the Atlantic to land on the American continent, and there were one or two remarkable migrations across the Pacific, until the fifteenth century the shipping of the world was generally coastal or limited to such landlocked seas as the Mediterranean. The breakthrough in ship design which, in the late fifteenth century, produced for the first time vessels which could sail anywhere, was obviously of the utmost significance if only because the world's surface is three-quarters ocean and only one-quarter land.

In the fifteenth century men had only the vaguest ideas of world geography. Educated men knew that the world was round, but only the most tenuous idea, if any, existed that an enormous continent lay across the Atlantic westwards from Europe. The very name 'Indian', applied to the indigenous inhabitants of the American continent, indicates how the early European arrivals thought they had reached India. Uneducated men, including seamen, believed that the world 'ended' somewhere in mid-Atlantic in a region of storms and of water rushing into a fathomless abyss.

The first European explorers

The pioneer work of European exploration of the rest of the world was not British. The first outstanding figure was the Portuguese, Prince Henry the Navigator, who in the late fifteenth century sponsored exploration down the west coast of Africa. Subsequently the Portuguese sailed right around Africa and established trading relations with India. The Italian, Christopher Columbus, under Spanish sponsorship, crossed the Atlantic in 1492 and discovered the West Indies. The actual name of America comes from another Italian, Amerigo Vespucci, who was supposed, probably falsely, to have been the first man to discover the American mainland in 1497. Yet another Italian, John Cabot, obtained English sponsorship for a voyage in which he discovered Newfoundland and confirmed the existence of the North American continent. The Portuguese, Ferdinand Magellan, led the first expedition to sail around the world, although he did not himself live to complete the voyage.

The two countries to set up overseas empires on the basis of the new discoveries were Spain and Portugal. In 1493 Pope Alexander VI partitioned the 'New World' between them on an east-west basis. This meant that Spain had most of America and Portugal had eastern Brazil plus as much of Africa and India as it could obtain. The English were allowed no share and did not, at the time, make any complaint.

Elizabethan seamen

English seamen appeared prominently on the scene during the reign of Queen Elizabeth I. This was nearly a century after the first major discoveries, and by then the Spanish and Portuguese colonial empires had settled into stable patterns. It was a particularly chaotic period in English history. Within just over 150 years England was to experience four changes of dynasty, a period as a republic and at least six changes in its official religion; one reigning monarch and one heir to the throne were executed. The record in the associated kingdom of Scotland in the same period was nearly as stormy.

Elizabeth I, a strong-willed but sometimes indecisive woman who never married, reigned for forty-five years of this difficult period. By birth she was illegitimate and thus, strictly, not entitled to hold the throne at all (in 1570 Pope Pius V issued a proclamation to depose her). The regime she led was essentially a party one, representing moderate Protestantism, and it was frequently in danger of being overthrown by internal and external enemies. However, Elizabeth employed ministers of high ability, maintained an elaborate secret police and, on occasion, showed calculated ruthlessness in dealing with enemies. Above all, during her long career, she managed to tap a feeling of national patriotism and to identify herself with it.

Elizabeth had little interest in empire-building and gave her seamen only cautious encouragement. Her main interests were the consolidation of her regime in England, the subjugation of Ireland and the religious-nationalistic civil wars in the Netherlands. But she did, as a sideline, enjoy collecting a share in the profits of overseas expeditions and eventually, when Philip of Spain tried to invade England, her sailors defeated him.

The Elizabethan seamen were an aggressive, able breed who at best were parasites on the established Spanish and Portuguese colonies, and at worst pirates. The only theoretical justification for their freebooting activities was that the pope had had no right to grant away the New World as the monopoly of particular countries. The English ruling class, after chopping and changing, had largely adopted the Protestant side in the controversies of the Reformation and thus was the more ready to challenge the pope's action. However, France, which remained mainly Catholic, was equally eager to break the Spanish-Portuguese monopoly.

The Spaniards' idea of colonialism was to mine as much gold and silver as they could, with the aid of slave labour, and transport it to their homeland so that they would be rich. The result was to ruin the monetary system of Spain and of Europe generally. With plentiful supply, the value of precious metals fell and there was a century-long inflation which was to be of the utmost advantage to business enterprises but bad for the common people. The occasional waylaying and capturing of the Spanish treasure fleets by English and French pirates was probably, in the long run, good for Spain because it helped to spread the monetary chaos.

The Spanish found the indigenous population of central America unsuitable for slavery: the people would not work hard and died off when punished. Accordingly the Spanish captured Negroes off the coast of Africa and transported them to slavery in their American colonies. Thus began the three centuries of the African slave trade, which weakened the continent and led to social problems which still vex the twentieth century. At the time, however, there was nothing particularly novel in it. Slavery and slave raiding were among the oldest human occupations – some Christians tried to rationalise the process by claiming that the victims were being converted from 'savagery' to 'true religion'. Long before the Europeans did so the Arabs had been carrying on a slave trade with Africa. There was even some slave trading in a European context. It was not unknown for British pirates to raid the coast of Italy and sell to the Turks Italians whom they had captured. Until the eighteenth century Algiers was the centre of the 'Barbary corsairs' who captured everyone they could for slavery.

The important factors about the African slave trade were its enormous size and the sheer volume of human suffering that it entailed. The slaves were crammed, lying down, in tiers in the ship's hold, and it was normal for twenty per cent of a cargo to die on a crossing. Later improvements reduced this 'wastage'; for example, it was found that slaves survived better if they were allowed up on deck, in relays, to take exercise.

Left: *Christopher Columbus, whose voyages to the New World presented Spain with the beginnings of a new empire.*

Right: *an Elizabethan galleon. The basis of England's continuing sea-power was firmly laid in the sixteenth century. In the years before the Armada the navy was re-organised and considerably enlarged by John Hawkins, until by 1558 it was among the most powerful in the world.*

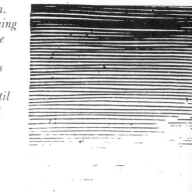

Left: *Philip II of Spain who, until the defeat of the Armada, was a constant threat to the Elizabethan throne. By the beginning of Elizabeth's reign Spain and Portugal already owned considerable overseas empires on the basis of their new discoveries.*

John Hawkins

The Spanish maintained a complete monopoly of all trade, including, since they wished to fully exploit their colonies, the slave trade. As always with a monopoly, prices tended to be unnecessarily high, and so any keen businessman who could break it would be sure of good profits. The first Englishman to seize upon this possibility was John Hawkins, who belonged to a prosperous business family at Plymouth in Devonshire. Hawkins found that he could fit out expeditions to Africa, capture slaves and, breaking the Spanish embargo, sell them in the Spanish colonies. His prices were lower than those of the official monopolists but, even so and despite many shipwrecks and disasters, he made money.

Supported by investments from fellow merchants and ultimately from the queen herself, Hawkins conducted three major slave-trading voyages. His technique for acquiring slaves was the simplest possible: he just cruised along the west coast of Africa, raided every village he saw and carried off those whom

he wanted. The English laughed at the tiny African bows and arrows, so toy-like compared with the English longbow, but later found that they were poisoned and that eight out of ten men hit by them afterwards died. Hawkins himself was hit but attributed his survival to having rubbed his wound with garlic.

Disposing of the cargo in the Americas was more difficult than gathering it in Africa. The Spanish colonists were, on the whole, anxious to buy Hawkins's slaves, but to do so meant defying their own king. Hawkins, besides being an excellent practical seaman and a good leader, seems to have been a skilled diplomat. In order to prevent the Spanish ambassador in London complaining to Queen Elizabeth, he insisted upon always getting a 'licence' to trade from the local Spanish governor. His first move, normally, on arriving at a Spanish settlement, was to send a letter to the governor with a blatant offer of a bribe. 'If you may,' he wrote to one governor, 'I most instantly desire you that you will take the pains to come hither that I might confer with you myself; truly it would be liefer to me than 10,000

ducats.' Hawkins also stressed that King Philip II of Spain had, through his marriage to Queen Mary I, been nominally king of England, and thus Hawkins was almost a Spanish compatriot. He spoke Spanish well, which helped considerably, and gave the impression that he was a Roman Catholic.

Sometimes such methods worked. In one place, Hawkins and the local governor arranged a complete mock battle, with Hawkins's ships firing into the jungle behind the township and his landing party 'advancing' into it to meet a Spanish group carrying a 'flag of truce'. The purpose of this play-acting was to enable the governor to write home to Spain to say that he had given the trading licence under duress. On other occasions the fighting was genuine and Hawkins conducted more or less forced trade, the governor buying off his attacks by granting a licence. On his third expedition Hawkins ran into a sizeable Spanish force and suffered such casualties that he returned to England having lost eighty per cent of his crew and five ships of his squadron of seven.

The queen made him treasurer of the Royal Navy, in which capacity he developed the characteristically British type of warship—a relatively small, highly manoeuvreable vessel with big guns which could blast its opposing galleon before the traditional hand-to-hand fighting took place between boarding parties. In the English navy the distinction between the 'soldiers', who did the fighting, and the 'sailors', who ran the ship, was rapidly obliterated: the new type of fighting seaman was the basis of the country's future maritime power. The Spanish Armada, sent to invade England, was defeated by the superior English ships and seamen—as well as bad weather—and this was largely Hawkins's work.

In his prime, Hawkins was England's leading seaman, but his reputation was rapidly overshadowed by that of his kinsman, his junior by ten years, Francis Drake.

Francis Drake

Drake, another Devonian, was born about 1545, the son of a

Protestant preacher who was eventually ordained in the Church of England. Many foreigners, especially the Spanish, have been unable to see in him more than a glorified pirate. He has, however, always been celebrated by his countrymen as a national hero, the process reaching its peak in nineteenth-century romanticism, such as that of Henry Newbolt, who wrote about Drake's legendary promise to come back to life if England were ever in danger:

Take my drum to England, hang et by the shore
Strike et when your power's runnin' low;
If the Dons sight Devon, I'll quit the port o' Heaven,
An' drum them up the Channel as we drummed them long ago.

Drake was a short, deep-chested man with red hair, ambitious, opportunistic, but on the whole humane. He had the strongest Protestant convictions – during piratical expeditions he held compulsory prayers twice a day for his crew – and he hated the Spanish Roman Catholics. Since he counted the papists as fair game, he was able to pile up a millionaire's fortune by raiding them without being disturbed by a troubled conscience. Such a combination of business acumen and idealism was characteristic of many later British empire builders, though in many ways Drake was the most distinctive. There are some obscurities in his life and background, but he appears to have been apprenticed to the sea at the age of twelve, and he sailed on Hawkins's expeditions. He acquired a practical and theoretical mastery of navigation and ship management and was a most effective leader of men.

John Hawkins, chief architect of the Elizabethan navy. Hawkins was the first Englishman to break the Spanish monopoly of the slave trade; his activities as an unlicensed trader, as well as Drake's piratical raids on the Spanish colonies, both played an important part in the long quarrel with Spain.

In 1572, when about twenty-seven, Drake set off with two ships, the size of modern pleasure yachts, to plunder the Spanish colonies in America. Unlike Hawkins, who maintained at least the formal fiction that he was a trader, Drake intended to seize whatever he could. The Spanish colonies lay wide open to attack, no serious defences having been considered necessary. At this time England and Spain were not yet at war and the only justification for Drake's piracy was that he was seeking revenge for injustices inflicted upon British traders captured by the Spaniards. It was also an age in which a man's religious beliefs really mattered. Captured Protestants were handed over to the Spanish Inquisition, which sent the younger ones for compulsory instruction in monasteries, and tortured and flogged the older ones preparatory to burning them at the stake or condemning them to serve as galley slaves.

Drake was incensed by such occurrences, and thought that they entitled him to behave in any manner he chose towards the Spanish. He established himself in a concealed natural harbour in the Isthmus of Panama, and with considerable verve set about plundering the colonies. With only eighty men he landed and attacked the major Spanish settlement of Nombre de Dios, a town the size of Plymouth, and nearly captured its treasury before being driven out. He seized an enormous treasure ship by the simple expedient of boarding her at night and battening the crew below hatches. Wounds and disease reduced his crew and it was with only thirty men that he landed to intercept the mule trains that were bringing Spanish treasure to the coast.

On the way, he caught a glimpse of the Pacific for the first time by climbing a tree. He was the first Englishman ever to see that ocean and he at once determined to navigate it. As a contemporary account put it: 'Falling down there upon his knees, he implored the Divine assistance that he might, at some time or other, sail thither and make a perfect discovery of the same; and hereunto he bound himself with a vow.' But the immediate business was the treasure trains and, after many setbacks and difficulties, Drake eventually captured gold and silver worth about £45,000 in the values of the time. (In modern terms it would be the equivalent of £2,000,000 or more.) His original ships were now old and unseaworthy, and to make the Atlantic crossing back to Plymouth, Drake captured two Spanish vessels.

Drake was by no means the only English pirate operating in this way on the Spanish Main. Such figures as Raleigh, Frobisher and Grenville had done the same, and there were also Protestant French pirates. However, Drake's successes overshadowed those of everyone else and he became famous, attracting the interest of Queen Elizabeth herself. At first she sent Drake into hiding lest his prominent presence in England should annoy the Spanish. But after two years she appointed him leader of an expedition to exploit 'Terra Australis', a continent belied to stretch southwards from South America, from the Magellan Strait. Since there were no Spanish in 'Terra Australis', Elizabeth thought this legitimate. Drake's main interest was sailing into the Pacific in order to plunder the Spanish from that side, and he may well have doubted whether 'Terra Australis' existed. However, he accepted the royal commission and, with finance put up by the queen, by London and Plymouth merchants and by himself, fitted out a fleet of five ships, of which the flagship was the hundred-ton *Pelican*, later renamed *Golden Hind*. As a security precaution, the crews were recruited on the understanding that the voyage was to be to the Middle East.

Drake made a long and difficult Atlantic crossing and had trouble with his crew. Things came to a head when he accused a gentlemanly officer, Thomas Doughty, of mutiny. Although Doughty had been Drake's close friend, Drake condemned him

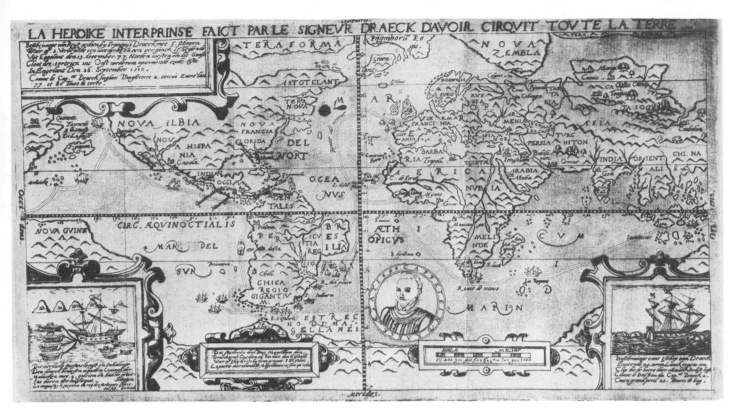

to death and had him beheaded. There is some mystery about the incident, but Drake seems to have been acting legitimately and Doughty seems to have accepted the justice of the sentence. Before the execution the two men first took Holy Communion together and then dined together to bid each other farewell.

When they reached the southern extremity of South America two ships were sent home and the remaining three entered the incredibly dangerous waters of the Magellan Strait, which nobody had navigated since Magellan himself fifty-eight years earlier. Violent winds and tides sweep through this rock-strewn channel, which at its narrowest is less than a mile wide, with towering cliffs on either side. It took Drake sixteen days to get through and then gales blew his fleet southwards, completely destroying one of the ships. The remaining pair discovered the true southward tip of the South American continent, Cape Horn, and established that 'Terra Australis' did not exist. Then one ship, with its crew in a semi-mutinous condition, broke off and fled back to England. Drake, with only the *Golden Hind*, turned towards sunnier Pacific waters further north where there were Spaniards to be plundered.

Drake's appearance on the west coast of America took the Spaniards completely by surprise. They themselves had never made the sea voyage around the continent and such ships as they had on the Pacific had been built on the west coast. They thought themselves completely secure from foreign pirates. Drake's major success was to capture a treasure ship with gold, silver and jewels of such colossal value as to be almost impossible to compute in modern terms. It must have been the equivalent of at least £10,000,000 and possibly much more. Drake crammed the *Golden Hind* with the stolen treasure; he now only needed somehow to get back to England for the expedition to show a gigantic profit for every investor from the queen downwards.

His first idea was to return by the 'north-west passage', a fabulous route that was supposed to run from the Pacific to the Atlantic somewhere north of California. But he found that, with no break in the land, he was compelled to keep going northwards and when he arrived in the mists near to what is

Drake's circumnavigation of the globe, 1577–80, as charted on a Dutch map. One of the objects of the voyage was a plan to discover, and establish trading bases on, the legendary 'Terra Australis'. Drake was appointed leader of this expedition, which was financed by the queen, the wealthy merchants of London and Plymouth and Drake himself.

now Vancouver he decided to turn back rather than risk the loss of his treasure-laden ship in dangerous exploration.

The birth of the British Empire

Drake returned to California and beached his ship for repairs just north of what is now San Francisco. He made friends with the local Indians and gave them medical advice. According to his own account they were so impressed that they offered to make him their king. Drake, accordingly, annexed the territory to the crown of England, an action which marked the birth of the British Empire. He set up a brass tablet to commemorate the event and this, supposedly, was discovered in 1937. Perhaps the tablet is fraudulent, though scientific tests have not disproved it, but the wording is exactly right in style, and it is worth giving in full because it exemplifies the manner in which the British acquired, or like to think they acquired, the greater part of their future empire.

BEE IT KNOWNE UNTO ALL MEN BY THESE PRESENTS
JUNE 17 1579 BY THE GRACE OF GOD AND IN THE NAME
OF HERR MAJESTY QUEEN ELIZABETH OF ENGLAND AND HERR
SUCCESSORS FOREVER I TAKE POSSESSION OF THIS KINGDOM
WHOSE KING AND PEOPLE FREELY RESIGNE THEIR RIGHT AND
TITLE IN THE WHOLE LAND UNTO HERR MAJESTIES KEEPING
NOW NAMED BY ME AND TO BE KNOWNE UNTO ALL MEN AS
NOVA ALBION

FRANCIS DRAKE

This first British colony of 'Nova Albion' remained in active operation for only five weeks, the time it took Drake to prepare for the next stage of his voyage. He had decided to circumnavigate the entire globe and, with his Indian 'subjects' apparently mourning his departure, set off westwards with a trade wind behind him. In the East Indies he found Portuguese traders already active in the spice trade but he managed to sign treaties with two local rulers which were to be of some value as precedents when, fifty years later, the British began seriously to compete.

There was a perilous incident when the *Golden Hind*, with all its treasure, ran aground and was in danger of foundering. The chaplain, Francis Fletcher, remarked that this was divine punishment for Drake's treatment of Doughty. Drake, furious, held a solemn ceremony at which he 'excommunicated' Fletcher from the Church of England and he made him wear an armband with the inscription: 'Francis Fletcher, the falsest knave that liveth.' However, Drake's faith in his own rectitude must have been confirmed when a near-miraculous gust of wind lifted the ship off the rock.

The remainder of the voyage, across the Indian Ocean, around the Cape of Good Hope and up the Atlantic coast of Africa was uneventful, and after an absence of two years and ten months Drake arrived back in Plymouth. He was the first captain ever to have sailed around the world. His first question, when he met English fishermen off Plymouth, was: 'Is the queen alive and well?' This was not mere solicitous loyalty but a direct question about the nature of the regime that was awaiting him–anything could have happened during his long absence.

Drake's voyage round the world and a fortune stolen from Spain made him in some respects a national hero. Ballads and poems were made up about him and he was credited with miraculous powers. There was even a proposal to put the *Golden Hind* on top of St Paul's Cathedral in London. However, many of his fellow sea captains disliked him for his swaggering manners and boastfulness and for the government he was something of an embarrassment because he obviously endangered relationships with Spain, now grown all the mightier through having taken over Portugal.

On the queen's instructions, Drake's booty was taken from Plymouth by a train of mules with military escort to the Tower of London where, ostensibly, an inventory was to be made of it, with a view to its being returned to its rightful owners. In practice most or all of the treasure eventually found its way into the pockets of the investors in the enterprise. The queen, after a period of characteristic indecision, received Drake and spent six hours in conversation with him. Later she visited the *Golden Hind*, which had been brought round to Deptford, and instructed the French ambassador, who was also present, to knight Drake.

Newfoundland and Virginia

'Nova Albion', the colony Drake had annexed, was important to him and he liked to boast about it. However, to Elizabeth and her government it seemed of little importance–they were preoccupied with the war in the Netherlands, with Ireland and with the threat of war with Spain. The next British attempts to found colonies were hardly more substantial. They were carried out by two half-brothers, Sir Humphrey Gilbert and Sir Walter Raleigh, adventurous courtiers of Elizabeth. In 1583 Gilbert sailed to Newfoundland and claimed it for the English crown, since it formed a useful base for fisheries. However, his ship sank with all hands on the return voyage. Although, on the basis of Gilbert's action Newfoundland has traditionally been reckoned as 'Britain's oldest colony', possession was for many years disputed by France and the British title was not completely established until 1713.

Raleigh wanted to form a settlement on the North American mainland, to the north of the Spanish colonies. It was to be called 'Virginia' in honour of the unmarried queen. Although he had in his time made bold voyages to the Americas, Raleigh did not take up direct leadership of the project but remained as the organiser in London. First, in 1584, he sent out two ships on an exploratory mission and they found what they regarded as suitable land on what is now the coast of North Carolina. The following year Raleigh sent out about a hundred men as settlers, with a governor, Ralph Lane, but they were beset by difficulties. Their stores ran out, their crops failed and they pined for home. After a year, Drake, on a further freebooting expedition against the Spaniards, called on them and at their request took them back to England.

In 1587 Raleigh made a third attempt to found 'Virginia' on the same spot. Women as well as men must go, he decided, if the settlement were to be a success, and the new expedition included seventeen women, two of them pregnant, and nine children. This colony on Roanoke Island totally vanished and nobody has ever discovered what happened to it.

Partly for religious reasons and partly because of English piracy, Philip II of Spain, Europe's most powerful monarch, decided to occupy England, and a huge fleet, the Armada, was dispatched for this purpose. In order to defend themselves, the English raised a fleet which was placed under the command of Lord Howard of Effingham, an intelligent politician but an inexperienced sailor. The real directing force was Drake, who was made vice-admiral. Undoubtedly the arrival of the Armada set off a wave of patriotic feeling in England and a determination to do down the foreigner which long remained a national characteristic. Beacons blazed across the land as the Armada came into sight. Howard and Drake, according to a legend which could be true, were at the time playing bowls on Plymouth Hoe. Drake remarked, 'There is time enough to finish the game and beat the Spaniards too.'

At sea, the outnumbered English fleet refused to obey convention by attempting to board the Spanish invaders: instead they blasted at them from a distance. They then sent in fireships, and the Spaniards scattered in a panic. Finally a gale drove the Spaniards up the North Sea–'God breathed and they were scattered' was one English account–and they made their way back home around the north of Scotland and along the west coast of Ireland. Spanish casualties reached nearly fifty per cent.

The repulse of the Spanish Armada established the reality of English sea power. The surge of patriotism it evoked helped to build the roistering national self-confidence which was to inspire the future empire.

However, it was not all gain. As a result of piratical attacks, the Spanish had strengthened their colonial defences and it was no longer so easy to seize treasure as when Drake was young. Drake himself found this when, with Hawkins, he set off on his final expedition to the West Indies in 1595. Both men suffered reverse after reverse and ultimately died of illness at sea. Piracy continued for another two centuries on the Spanish Main, throwing up such characters as Captain Teach and Captian Kidd. For a time the Bahamas were actually administered by pirates, who elected their own governor.

However, with the end of Drake's career, piracy became more desperate and more definitely an occupation for outcasts – a footnote to history rather than part of the mainstream. The future for Britain was to lie not in raiding other people's colonies but in setting up its own. By the end of the sixteenth century Pope Alexander VI's division of the New World between Spain and Portugal had for every practical purpose become obsolete. England, France and the Netherlands established a new principle that they were entitled to make colonies in any territory that was not already occupied by Christians. The Spanish and

Portuguese tacitly accepted this and made no further attempt to maintain a monopoly of the whole American continent.

Henry Hudson

The greatest English seaman in the generation after Drake was not a pirate but an explorer, Henry Hudson. A man of implacable will, Hudson first attempted to find a route from England to China by way of the Arctic regions. He reached a bitterly cold area of continual darkness with storms driving his ship towards the ice-cap of the world. The crew heard the terrible sound of the sea pounding against the ice, and they had to pull their ship clear by rowing. On a subsequent voyage under Dutch sponsorship, Hudson became the first English captain to see what is now New York. He surveyed the superb harbour, sailed 150 miles inland up the Hudson River, named after him, and reached what is now Albany, the capital of New York State, in 1609. In 1613, as a result of his reports, the Dutch established the colony of New Amsterdam which, half a century later, was captured by the British and renamed New York.

Hudson's final voyage, in 1610, was again in Arctic waters off what is now north-eastern Canada. He discovered the Hudson Strait and sailed into the enormous expanse of Hudson's Bay, 900 miles across at its widest point. There his ship was locked during the winter, and when the thaw came in the spring of 1611 his crew refused to obey his orders for further exploration. They marooned him in a boat and set off back to England. The last anyone saw of Hudson was a dwindling figure staring steadily at his ship as it sailed away from him.

Hudson's work helped to make it plain that north of the Spanish and Portuguese colonies lay what now is virtually the whole territory of the United States and Canada, ready and open for European colonisation.

In 1583 Sir Humphrey Gilbert annexed Newfoundland, which formed a useful base for fisheries, in the name of the queen. During the next thirty years several attempts were made to colonise the island, though Gilbert's ship sank with all hands on the return voyage.

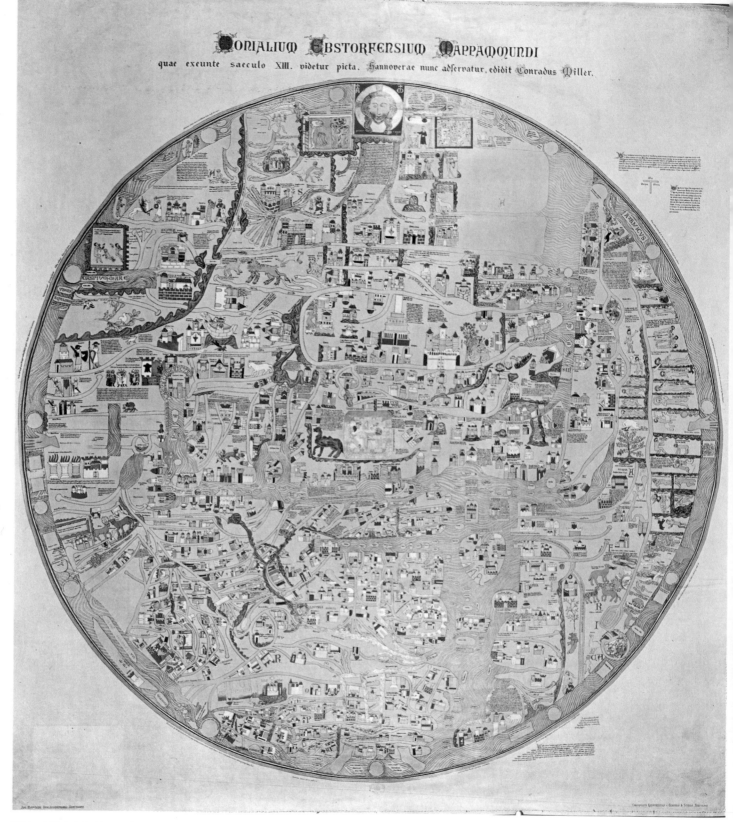

*This delightful thirteenth-century map from north-west Germany
demonstrates how scanty geographical knowledge was before the time
of Mercator, when map-makers were still basing their work on the
ancient world of Ptolemy.*

By the sixteenth century new instruments such as astrolabes had speeded up navigation and exploration; sea voyages were still hazardous, but the mariner was less likely to become hopelessly lost as soon as he was out of sight of land. Here an astrolabe is being used to measure latitude.

Elizabeth I of England. Although the great English voyages of discovery were begun in the reign of Elizabeth I, she herself was not particularly interested in empire-building, and her seamen received little support or encouragement from her. However, the surge of patriotism that sprang up during her reign must have played its part in the awakening of the voyaging impulse. So, no doubt, did simple greed—the Elizabethan seamen were not noted for the purity of their motives.

Left: *Raleigh's attempts to found the colony of Virginia on Roanoke Island were unsuccessful. The first landing (below) was made in 1584, and a year later he sent out a hundred men with a governor. These first colonists begged to be returned home, and a further expedition sent in 1587, which included women and children, vanished without trace.*

One of the direct results of the discoveries of Henry Hudson was the establishment of the Hudson's Bay Company, giving England its first foothold in Canada. The lower illustration shows part of the charter granted in 1670 by Charles II to: 'the Governor and Company of Adventurers of England Trading into Hudson's Bay'. The charter also gave power to the company to rule according to English law within its territory.

Sir Walter Raleigh, one of the great seamen and explorers of the Elizabethan Age. He was the founder of the colony of Virginia but his later career, blighted by the dislike of James I, was frought with disappointment and ended in tragedy.

The defeat of the Spanish Armada, 1588. The repulse of Philip II's 'invincible Armada' by the much smaller but more agile British fleet under Drake and Hawkins served both to strengthen English patriotism and to establish the reality of England's sea power.

The first colonists

Penn's treaty with the Indians.
As a haven for his fellow
Quakers, who were being
subjected to severe persecution,
Penn asked for and was granted
a tract of land as payment of a
debt owed by Charles II to his
father. The grant was signed in
1681, and Penn was made
master of the province of
Pennsylvania. He allowed
complete religious tolerance, was
conciliatory to the Indians, and
encouraged the formation of
companies to work the new
colony.

The British, the French and the Dutch began the colonisation of the North American continent almost simultaneously. There were also some very small settlements of Danes and Swedes. All newcomers regarded it as empty territory in which the existing Indian population had few or no rights. They could see in the Indians nothing that resembled a settled state or government, as they knew it, and, in any event, felt morally entitled to settle in any territory not ruled by a Christian prince. Certainly there was plenty of room for the newcomers. Today the United States and Canada, between them, support a population of over 200 million people, and there still seems to be ample room available. In the seventeenth century, when European colonisation began, there were probably fewer than one million Indians in the same area. Initially the British tended to patronise the Indians, to regard them as unspoiled children of nature whose innocence should be admired and ignorance instructed. But, not surprisingly, quarrels arose between particular groups of settlers and some of the Indian tribes, and there were bitter complaints about the Indians' alleged treachery. The French colonisers, especially the Jesuit missionaries, established better relations with the Indians.

The French were the first permanent settlers when they established Acadia (Nova Scotia) in 1604. From there the soldier Samuel de Champlain struck inland and founded and named the city of Quebec. In 1612 the French government set about officially building the 'New France' in Canada, with Champlain as the first governor. Quebec has always since been solidly French in population but Acadia alternated between British and French control until 1713, when the British acquired it for good. Three years after the French had settled in Acadia, the British started the colony of Virginia. This was on the same site as modern Virginia and had nothing to do with Sir Walter Raleigh's abortive Virginia project a hundred miles farther south.

The Dutch came on the scene with the establishment of New Amsterdam (New York) in 1613 but, although they colonised with great energy, they failed to obtain a lasting political hold. New Amsterdam became British by annexation, but the future of the continent was to depend on the final outcome of a century and half's contest between the British and French. However, Dutch names have always been prominent among the American upper classes and it is still held to be a sign of smart breeding to have the Dutch prefix 'van' in one's name. Four American presidents – van Buren, Hoover and the two Roosevelts – have born names of Dutch origin.

The founding colony

Virginia, the 'old dominion', can be considered as a portent of the future gigantic expansion of the British people and their language in new continents across the world. Today it is a relatively quiet part of the United States but it has had a stirring past – it provided five of the country's first ten presidents and it was the principal battle ground of the American Civil War. Its official name, 'Commonwealth of Virginia' and not 'State of Virginia', is an echo of its sixteenth-century past. The original settlement, in what was to be characteristic manner, was sponsored by a commercial company charted by the British crown. King James I, who had united in his person the English and Scottish crowns on the death of Elizabeth I, granted the charter in 1606 and the following year 105 colonists, all men, landed in Chesapeake Bay and named their first township Jamestown in honour of the king.

At first there was no certainty that the colony would survive. Raleigh's Virginia had been a fiasco and it looked as if the new colony might well go the same way. Strange diseases – 'swelling, fluxes, burning fevers' – attacked them causing so many deaths that it was difficult for the survivors to keep up the burials. Their crops failed and they would have died of famine had not a local tribe of Indians given them some food. But relations with the Indians were strained, and led sometimes to fighting, in which more settlers were killed.

After two years the remnant was on the point of giving up when a ship arrived with fresh colonists and supplies from England. To the fore came the jaunty personality of Captain John Smith, who must rank as one of the greatest empire builders. He was only twenty-six but already, before joining the Virginia expedition, he had, by his own account, served in three European armies, had been thrown into the sea as a heretic, been the slave of a Turkish nobleman and had fought as a kind of gladiator for the Turks. Smith was, as he put it himself, determined not to die of famine and he urged the settlers on to till the ground and build houses. At the same time he negotiated with the Indians, using a combination of force and trade to try to make them useful to the colony. As a defensive precaution he drilled the whole population and gave them military instruction on a piece of ground he called Smithfield (one of the joys of early colonisation everywhere was that of giving names to geographical features).

The community was, however, a highly neurotic one, and absurd suspicions grew up that Smith was really a traitor in league with the Indians. On one trip into the interior he was captured by an Indian tribe and, although he gave them theological and astronomical instruction, they decided to execute him. At the last moment, however, the chief's beautiful daughter, Pocahontas, interceded successfully for him. She later came to England, was received at court and married an Englishman.

Back in the colony the remaining settlers – there were now less than 40 of the original 105 – decided that Smith was indeed a traitor, and when he returned after three weeks with the Indians he was condemned to be hanged. However, a shift in the balance of power saved him and he resumed his leadership. Without Smith, Virginia would probably have perished in its early years.

In fact the colony did come to the very brink of extinction. On hearing that a governor was to be sent out from London to take charge, Smith left and returned home in 1609. The ship that took him had brought a fresh reinforcement of settlers but even this new blood could not make the colony viable. In 1610 the formal decision was taken to abandon Virginia and the survivors embarked for home. As they sailed down the James River towards the sea, however, they met three well-stocked ships from England and with them the new governor, appointed for life, Lord de la Warr. The colony started again and, gradually groped its way towards stability. By 1618 there were ten townships: churches had been built, crops were growing and families had started.

The first parliament

In the same year the Virginia Company granted the colony a written constitution by which the inhabitants were to elect a general assembly consisting of two 'burgesses' from each township. This assembly, with the consent of the governor and his council, was empowered to make laws. Thus there came into existence the first parliament on the American continent, and from the start it was a vigorous one. It has met at regular intervals continuously up to the present day.

Thus even at this very early stage the British were extending to their overseas empire the same principle of legislation by debate in parliament that they used at home. Indeed, this principle operated in Virginia long before it was completely established in London, since it required the civil war in the middle of

the seventeenth century to force the English parliament defini-
tively into the constitution. In almost every territory they ever
acquired the British set up legislative assemblies. In the 'white'
colonies these tended to be elected, and in Africa and India they
were for a long time nominated, but the idea of legislation by
debate was the same. The elected legislatures were to be the
mechanism for the ultimate dissolution of the British Empire –
the break-up came early and suddenly in the case of the United
States, and rather more gradually, in the mid-twentieth century,
in the modern Commonwealth.

In the seventeenth century the tendency on the mainland of
Europe was to move away from parliamentary-type institutions
and for kings to become more autocratic. That Britain went in
the opposite direction may be considered by many to be an
important service to the world. Of course, in the long run an
elected local assembly could never run in harmony with an
executive government appointed from London, but in the
seventeenth century this kind of problem was not much
considered.

The status of Virginia as the founding colony of the British
Empire in North America has rarely been properly celebrated,
except by the Virginians themselves. The true origin of the
American empire is commonly, although incorrectly, held to
have been the establishment of New England and the colony of
Massachusetts by the Pilgrim Fathers in 1620. However, in all
but precedence the Pilgrim Fathers were true founders because
they initiated a movement which was to bring something
approaching mass immigration to America and a vital ingredi-
ent in what was to become the American way of life.

The Pilgrim Fathers

The Pilgrim Fathers were English Puritans, that is, extreme
products of the Protestant Reformation. They saw this world as
the immediate ante-chamber to the next, and thought that their
whole way of life should be based upon religious considerations,
with great attention paid to prayer and moral living. They
believed in the utmost simplicity. Nowadays it is almost impossible to realise the importance that religion had in the seventeenth century. The German Thirty Years War and the English
civil wars were fought primarily for religious reasons, and both
Drake and the Spaniards had had the strongest religious
motivations. Nothing incongruous was seen in a man being
willing to die or to kill for some detail of religious belief or
practice.

For the Puritan wing in England, an energetic minority, the
Church of England, as established by Elizabeth I, was not
sufficiently Protestant. One reaction, besides fighting inside
England, was to dream of founding a new Puritan Commonwealth in the New World across the Atlantic. Indeed, it was
commonly held that God had especially provided North
America for this purpose. During the seventeenth century some
40,000 English people migrated to America – something like one
per cent of the total population. The overwhelming majority of
them did so in pursuit of the Puritan dream (Oliver Cromwell
himself nearly went), and they built up the American colonies
from isolated outposts into a settled way of life.

The Pilgrim Fathers were the first such group; originally they
consisted of dissenters from the established church in Scrooby,
Nottinghamshire, and Gainsborough, Lincolnshire. The two
groups joined forces and migrated to the Netherlands where
they were able to practise their religion without interference.
However, after ten years they began to fear that they would lose
their English identity and, after prayer and fasting, they decided
to move to America and start a completely new country on their
own lines. The magnitude of this idea at that time is difficult to
comprehend. They were proposing, with their women and

children, to undertake a voyage, during which they might well
sink on the way, to an unknown continent inhabited by dangerous savages in which many previous colonisation attempts had
ended in disaster. But they wanted to build the City of God for
the English people, and America was the only possibility.
Accordingly they sent envoys to James I, who gave them a sort
of tacit connivance, and they obtained a patent from the
Virginia Company to settle in land which, vaguely, was within
its sphere of influence. They also raised capital for London
merchants, who were hoping for a profitable fur trade.

The advance party of the Pilgrim Fathers was thirty-five
strong and they took into their ship, the *Mayflower*, a further
sixty-seven emigrants. However, the thirty-five from the Puritan
Church were the leaders, and remained as such when they
settled in New England. The *Mayflower* set sail from Southampton in September, 1620, with much singing of psalms and
shedding of tears, and, after a call at Plymouth, reached Cape
Cod after a two months voyage. Like the original Virginia
settlers many of these pioneers died of disease, but unlike the
Virginians they had women and children with them; in the first
six months they lost a third of their numbers. A contemporary
account refers to: 'The living scarce able to bury the dead; the
well not sufficient to tend the sick.' The graves were unmarked
to prevent the Indians from finding out how the colony was
diminishing. Probably for religious reasons, though, the New

The British, French and Dutch settlers in the North American continent regarded the Indian population with contempt, or at best amusement, and felt morally justified in appropriating their land. Not surprisingly, the Indians frequently took their revenge, as in this illustration, which shows Jesuits meeting their deaths at the hands of Iroquois Indians.

Samuel de Champlain, explorer, colonial pioneer, and first governor of French Canada. He founded the city of Quebec in July 1608. In 1629 Quebec was forced to surrender to the British, and he was taken to England as a prisoner. But he returned to his post when Canada was restored to the French, and died there in 1633.

The French were the first permanent settlers in Canada. This illustration from Champlain's Voyages shows a view of the Sainte Croix, the earliest French settlement in Acadia (Nova Scotia) established in 1604.

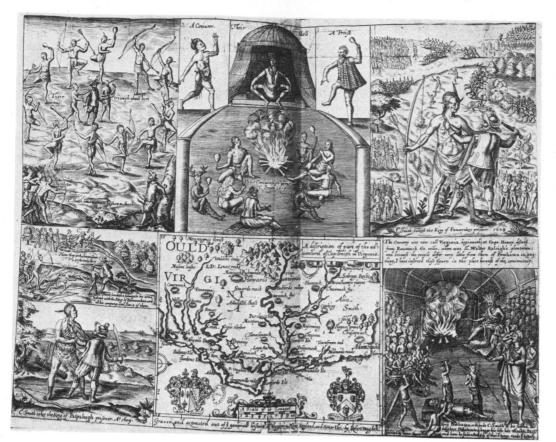

Englanders had better self-discipline and a stronger will to work than the first Virginians, and within a year of landing they were gathering their first harvest, for which they gave solemn thanksgiving to God. This was the first 'Thanksgiving Day' which has continued ever since as a major American festival.

During the next two decades a further 12,000 English Puritans settled in New England, some of them comprising complete congregations who came out with their ministers. They took the name 'New England' very literally and were fervently patriotic; they were building not a different country but a purified version of the old one. As one emigrant congregation caught their last glimpse of Land's End at the start of its Atlantic voyage, their minister, Francis Higginson, called some of them to the stern of the ship and told them: 'We will not say, as the Separatists were wont to say at their leaving of England, "Farewell Babylon! Farewell Rome!" But we will say, Farewell dear England! Farewell the church of God in England and all the Christian friends there! We do not go to New England as Separatists.'

The original Massachusetts colony spread out to further settlements at Connecticut, Maine, New Hampshire, Rhode Island and Vermont but except for Rhode Island they maintained a degree of unity as 'The New England Confederation of Bible Commonwealth', Massachusetts retained the leading position. The Dutch in New York called them the 'Jankes' (a derisive diminutive of Jan, the Dutch for John), and this word, corrupted into Yankee, became the regular nickname for New Englanders. The sprightly, self-sufficient Yankee, with his clipped accent – the accent made world famous in the middle of the twentieth century by the Kennedy family – became a most characteristic figure. Virtually all the original Yankees were of English stock.

Life in New England

Most New Englanders, for their first century, had little notion of political or religious liberty. There were elected legislatures, but full citizenship was confined to church members, who comprised only about twenty per cent of the adult male population. To become a church member involved a puritanical way of life and the ability to convince the church elders that one had been 'elected' to salvation. Rival religious sects were not tolerated. People who tried to set them up were flogged and even hanged – by the end of the century Quakers were being hanged in Boston, Salem and Massachusetts. Salem also suffered a wave of hysteria over witchcraft and, to doleful sermons from the ministers, supposed witches were led out to be hanged from a tree. It is only fair to recall, however, that in Britain at this time there were still cases of witches being burned at the stake, albeit with gunpowder tied to their necks to reduce their suffering.

The penal code covered sexual offences, with fornicators and adulterers being whipped, imprisoned and put in the stocks. The general aim was to get girls and boys married off soon after puberty, both to reduce sexual misdemeanors and to provide new homesteads and families to strengthen the community. The young couple carried on their courtship in bed, in the practice known as 'bundling', with their clothes sewn up to prevent too close a contact. The point of 'bundling' was that it was only in the warmth and privacy of bed that a couple could get to know one another – otherwise little privacy was available.

As the settlements struck inland, more and more land became available and the pioneer could set up his own farm for only the labour of clearing the virgin bush. Technically the land was held to belong to the king, who was farming it out to the settlers, and the Indians were held to have no property rights. Naturally the Indians did not accept this view and the settlements were exposed to Indian raids, with New Englanders scalped or carried off to be tortured to death. On their side the New Englanders were equally brutal. They regarded their land as the gift of God. The preachers saw the Indians as cruel, pagan savages who paid little or no attention to Christian dogma and from their pulpits proclaimed a holy war against them. In 1637 there was a full-scale war against the Pequot Indians with wholesale massacres and then a general Indian 'rising' in 1670.

However there was some reaction against the puritanical totalitarianism. Connecticut was founded by a group that wanted rather more freedom than was allowed in Massachusetts. Then a democrat, Roger Williams, appeared. He claimed equal rights for all, and even that the Indians were the legitimate owners of the land. This was regarded as heresy and, after trial before a church court, he was banished. Williams went to Rhode Island where he befriended the Indians and, with other white dissenters, founded a new settlement which for long stood a little aloof from the rest of America.

Maryland and Pennsylvania

Adjacent to New England, but of an entirely different type, was the proprietary colony of Maryland. It belonged to Lord Baltimore, a former English Secretary of State who had become a Roman Catholic, and until the War of Independence, Baltimore and his successors reigned over it almost as kings. Baltimore acquired the territory, by permission of Charles I, largely as a refuge for Roman Catholics, who were still being persecuted in England.

The name 'Maryland' came, officially, from Charles's queen, Henrietta Maria, but there may well also have been some purely religious motive in it. So feared and disliked were the Roman Catholics in English ruling circles that there could be no question of giving them a religious monopoly as the Puritans had in New England or, for that matter, the Anglicans almost had in Virginia. The only method was to allow religious toleration and so, in 1634, Maryland came into existance on a basis of freedom of worship for all Christians. But even liberal Maryland would not tolerate non-Christians – the relevant legislation ran: 'No person professing to believe in Jesus Christ shall from henceforth be any waies troubled or discountenanced.' In the usual manner, Baltimore established an elected legislature for his subjects.

Half a century later came another colony of a somewhat similar type. William Penn, son of a royalist admiral, had become

Top: *the landing of the Pilgrim Fathers at Plymouth on 22 December 1620. Plymouth was the first permanent settlement of Europeans in New England.*

Above: Mayflower II, *a reconstruction of the famous* Mayflower *on which the original party of thirty-five Pilgrim Fathers, with sixty-seven other emigrants, set sail from Southampton in 1620.*

29

Of Florida.

Indians of Florida, painted by John White in 1587. White accompanied the first colonists to Roanoke Island and was commissioned by Raleigh to make drawings to attract new settlers. Although his vivid watercolours failed to achieve this object, they survive as authentic portrayals of the appearance and way of life of the pre-colonial inhabitants.

The residence of David Twining. This typical Pennsylvania farm was the boyhood home of the artisan-painter Edward Hicks. The Twinings, and Hicks himself, were staunch Quakers, and Hicks became a prominent minister who travelled at his own expense to preach.

a Quaker. He insisted on wearing his hat in the presence of King Charles II and addressed him, plainly, as 'Charles Stuart' instead of 'Your Majesty' or 'Sire'. The king was amused and rather admired Penn's courage. Since Quakers were being flogged and hanged in Massachusetts, Penn wanted to set up an American colony for them and, in payment of a debt owed by the king to his family, the king granted him a strip of land next to New York, which, along with what became Delaware, had been annexed by the British in 1664. Like Maryland the new colony allowed religious toleration, and was ruled by Penn and his descendants as proprietors.

Meanwile the British had conquered New Amsterdam from the Dutch and renamed it New York after the king's brother, the Duke of York. There followed colonisation in Raleigh's original 'Virginia' in territories named North Carolina and South Carolina, after the monarch.

Rivalry in North America

Thus within a century of the death of Francis Drake, there had come into existence a string of a dozen British colonies along the Atlantic seaboard of north America. The British had also seized various Caribbean islands, notably Barbados and Jamaica, and established in them a wealthy sugar industry based upon massive slave labour. It was at this time that the slave trade really developed as a major factor in both the British and American economies; humanitarian objections were non-existent – even such a figure as William Penn was a slave owner. By a bold, almost nonsensical, stroke, the British crown had claimed and granted by charter to the Hudson Bay Company the unknown empty expanses of northern Canada; the grant covered some two million square miles and to this day much of it is still not settled. Part of it, Alaska, was to be settled by Russians approaching from the opposite direction and not by

The expulsion of Quakers from Massachusetts, 1660. The first Quaker missionaries arrived in America between 1656 and 1658, and in spite of severe persecution for religious non-conformity in most of the colonies, they made many converts.

The building of Jamestown, Virginia. The charter for the founding colony in Virginia was granted by King James I in 1606, and the expedition landed in Chesapeake bay the following year. Had it not been for the indomitable Captain John Smith, the colony might have been as short-lived as Raleigh's, and indeed it did come very close to extinction.

the British at all; eventually the Russians sold Alaska to the United States. However in the long run, and after French power had been eliminated, the land of the Hudson's Bay Company was to be the essential area of expansion for the nineteenth century British Dominion of Canada.

But it was still by no means inevitable that North America would end up as an English-speaking continent. The Spanish, in addition to their large and well established empire in central and southern America, held California, Florida, Mexico and what became Texas. The French had their vigorous colony at Quebec and held Acadia (Nova Scotia) on the Canadian coast. French pioneers, notably La Salle, had also surveyed and claimed an enormous territory to the west of the British seaboard colonies and named it Louisiana after King Louis XIV. Had France ever really settled Louisiana it would not only have cut off the seaboard British colonies from westwards expansion but would also have become the major power on the North American continent. Today the area of the United States would be primarily French rather than English speaking.

Louisiana, in addition to the present state of that name, also included what became the states of Mississipi, Arkansas, Missouri, Nebraska, Iowa, South Dakota, part of north Dakota, Minnesota, Kansas, Oklahoma, Colorado and Wyoming. It was to take five wars before the issue was settled.

The weakness of the French as against the British was that they attracted comparatively few colonists. Quebec was peopled by a tough breed of French peasants mostly from Normandy but even there, after the initial impetus had passed, immigration tailed off to nothing. The French thought of their colonies in primarily political and strategic terms, as extensions of the power of their king. Everything was planned by the government. The British colonies, on the other hand, were the work of

enterprising and sometimes eccentric individuals who wanted to fashion their own way of life.

It used to be customary for writers to extol in the most romantic terms the strange urge in the British which drove them overseas to found new countries. It was held that there was some 'genius' or 'destiny' in the British 'race'. Curious parallels were drawn between migration into the empire and the migration of the original Anglo-Saxon tribes from Germany to England. However, even when allowances are made for exaggeration, it does seem that this was a particularly vital period in British history. The disorders and wars within Britain itself were a stimulus to migration. Indeed some migrants arrived in America more or less as slaves as punishment for being on the losing side – they could earn their freedom after a period of years. There were also many who voluntarily entered indentured jobs, to which they were bound for a period of years, as a means of getting started in the New World.

One aspect of British vitality was the mysterious explosion in the birth-rate. From the seventeenth to eighteenth centuries the British population doubled more or less every generation. Why this happened is unknown (improved sanitation and medicine exerted only the most marginal influence) but certainly the British Isles themselves became one of the most densely populated regions of the world, and, in addition, the British spilled over to provide the majority of the population of the United States, Canada, Australia and New Zealand, and to make an important contribution to white Africa.

However even as early as the beginning of the nineteenth century it was becoming incorrect to consider the inhabitants of the British American colonies as if they were purely British. A distinctive new type of person was arising, the American. He was someone who had never seen Europe and never expected to do so. He preserved in his accent the nasal twang of Elizabethan England, which the British themselves were losing. He worked hard and expected big rewards for doing so. Achievement was more important than status.

In strict law he was accounted a citizen of Middlesex, England, who happened to be living abroad, but in practice his loyalties were to his own community. He was probably staunchly Protestant. Although two universities had already been established – Harvard in Massachusetts and at Williamsburg in Virginia – he was likely to hold book-learning in some contempt and to prefer practical activities. The situation soon rectified itself but there was a shortage of professional men of all kinds except ministers in the second generation of American colonists. However, he was likely to be able to read and write, especially if he was a New Englander – elementary education in New England was better than in Britain. His book was the Bible, if he read at all. His parents might have gone through extreme hardship in building up a farm or business and quite possibly he had too. His outlook was probably parochial. Communications within the colonies were poor and between them almost nonexistent – the only way of travelling from one colony to another was by sea. Suggestions arose from time to time, especially from the British government, that the colonies should form some kind of central administration to look after such matters as defence. Such ideas broke down because of the parochial outlook of the colonists and the dislike of their legislatures for voting money. There were certain local militia forces, of doubtful efficiency, but the main burden of defence rested upon London. For all their love of independence, the colonists at this stage never thought it beneath their dignity to apply to London for help when things went wrong.

When eventually the colonies united and voted money to form their own army, it was to be not in support of the British Empire but in the desire to break away from it.

The fortified settlement built between the rivers Ashley and Cooper at Charleston, South Carolina. In 1670 English colonists, led by William Sayle, settled at Albemarle Point on the Ashley River; ten years later they moved to Oyster Point, where their capital, Charles Town, had been laid out. The city became the most important seaport in the southern colonies and a leading centre of wealth and culture.

Top right: it is not certain when the British connection with the island of Barbados began, but it is known that in about 1624 John Powell landed a party, and he inscribed on a tree the words, 'James K. of E. and of this Island'. This engraving shows sugar production in the early seventeenth century; the sugar trade assured the prosperity of the West Indies.

St George Towne
D

Warwicks forte
E

Right: *the Bermuda settlement, from Smith's* General Historie of Virginia. *The start of the Bermuda colony was quite accidental: in 1609 Sir George Somers, leading an expedition to Virginia, was shipwrecked there. The islands were included in the third charter of the Virginia company, who sent out sixty settlers to the new colony in* 1612.

The first sahibs

Sir Thomas Roe, first English ambassador at the court of the Moghul emperor. He and William Hawkins, an amusing conversationalist with whom the Emperor Jahangir struck up a friendship, were instrumental in obtaining protection for the English factory at Surat.

From the moment of the European discovery of the continent of America it was possible for the imaginative man to suppose that a great new empire could be built there and, indeed, empires were built very quickly. The Spanish Empire was a functioning force, operating on settled routines, only a century after Columbus's voyage. Within a century of their first settlements the British reached the verge of dominating the north American continent.

In the case of India and the East, however, there was no notion in the beginning that here the British Empire at its most magnificent was to be formed. When the British Empire reached its height in the early twentieth century as the greatest world power, three quarters of its population was in India. Hardly surprisingly nobody planned this – it was completely unforseeable and even in retrospect the root causes are difficult to identify fully.

When Europeans began their take-over of India in the fifteenth century there were few indications that they were technically superior. Like Europe, India had often been devastated by wars but in wealth, culture and sophistication of government it was in many ways superior. From India had come modern arithmetic and algebra – the so-called 'Arabic' numerals are really Indian. Certainly civilisation had a longer direct history in India than in Western Europe. So far as there were European technical superiorities they lay in sea-going ships and the will to sail them long distances. Possibly, too, the Europeans had some slight advantage in firearms, but none that the Indians could not quickly adopt. Of all the monarchs on earth, the emperor of China and the Moghul emperor of India ruled the largest and potentially the most powerful territories. In comparison the countries of Western Europe were small and in some ways even backward, their princes not to be compared in status to the emperors of the east. When King James I of Britain sent a letter to the emperor of India, the latter considered it beneath his dignity even to reply.

Early contacts with the East

Contacts between Asia and Europe had existed from prehistoric times and, although maps were deficient, educated men on both sides had an approximate idea of what the other was like. Trade routes running through what is now the south-western part of the Soviet Union had for uncountable centuries carried caravans of silks, spices and perfumes from Asia to Europe.

In the thirteenth century the Italian Polo family, including its best-known member Marco, had visited India and spent years in China. All that needed to be discovered to start the new phase was a way of reaching the Far East by sea and this happened in 1497 when the Portuguese Vasco da Gama became the first captain, so far as is known, to sail around the Cape of Good Hope and into the Indian Ocean. This was just five years after Columbus's first voyage to America and it must be more than coincidence that they both happened almost simultaneously – it had something to do with the strange new vitality that was stirring in Western Europe.

Under the pope's ruling of 1494, dividing between Spain and Portugal the whole non-Christian world, Portugal gained India and China. The Portuguese of course had no intention of conquering these countries – it would have been like a flea challenging two elephants – but only of trading with them. During the following century Portugal acquired, as trading posts, Goa in India and Macao in China on lease, both of them tiny in size. The sea route between the East and Europe was both quicker and cheaper than the old route and Portugal, with its monopoly, enjoyed the most prosperous century in its history. Unlike the Spaniards in America, the Portuguese traders were not troubled by Drake or other pirates.

Communications opened up, too, in the religious field. The Jesuits, the Roman Catholic religious society founded in the first flush of the Counter-Reformation, sent the Spanish Francis Xavier to India, Japan and China. In Japan, Xavier set up a Christian community which lasted for a century but then the Japanese rulers – wisely in view of what happened elsewhere – cut off almost all contacts with the outside world and remained isolated for two centuries.

The Merchant Adventurers

British probings to the east started in a different direction, towards Russia. The aim was partly to trade with Russia and partly to try to discover a north-east sea passage to Japan and China. Under the leadership of Sebastian Cabot, who had explored the coast of Brazil and was son of the discoverer of Newfoundland, a joint stock company was set up, the Company of Merchant Adventurers of London. It came, informally, to be known as the Muscovy Company, but the original idea was to trade with the Far East as well as Russia.

The formation of the company caused high excitement not only among City of London financiers and the government but also among the ordinary people – evidence, perhaps, of the zest for expansion that existed among the English even so early. When the company's first two ships set sail from the Thames in 1553 they fired their guns in celebration and people flocked to see them. 'The courtiers came running out and the common people flocked together, standing very thick upon the shore; the Privy Council, they looked out at the windows of the Court, and the rest ran up to the tops of the towers.' On the journey one ship was caught in ice and foundered with all hands, but the other reached Moscow and its captain, Richard Chancellor, was received in audience in the Kremlin by Tsar Ivan the Terrible. Although no navigable sea route to China could be found, a sound trading relationship was established with the Russians and some Englishmen moved permanently to Moscow to assist it, their families eventually intermarrying with Russians. There was of course never any idea of conquest.

The Merchant Adventurers had been formed on a 'joint stock' basis, that is, the members did not trade on their own account but pooled their capital so that the company operated as a single unit (the older type of company had been a mere association in which the members retained their own capital). The company's success in Russia encouraged others to follow a similar pattern of organisation. In particular, it was adopted when 200 London businessmen formed the East India Company which, arguably, was the most influential commercial company ever to have existed. It ended up as ruler of India.

The East India Company

The aged Queen Elizabeth I signed the charter of the East India Company on the last day of the sixteenth century. Its purposes, like those of the Merchant Adventurers, were simply to trade and to make money. If anyone had told the original directors that their employees would eventually conquer India it would have appeared hardly more improbable to them than if they had been told that an Indian shopkeeper would conquer England. Recognition of the fact that in the formative period of the British Empire, especially in the east, the only motive of the British was to do business and make money is essential for an understanding of the whole subject. Some business transactions might be legitimate and others brutal, but business was always the object. The enormous political consequences which ensued were, in the last resort, an unexpected side-effect. It can reasonably be argued that British rule brought advantages as well as hardships for the colonial peoples but the British motive, in the beginning, was to do neither, but simply to trade.

Sebastian Cabot, son of the discoverer of Newfoundland, who in 1553 became governor of a joint stock company, the Company of Merchant Adventurers of London. Although it later became known as the Muscovy Company, the original idea was to trade with the Far East as well as with Russia.

The Emperor Aurangzeb, whose disastrous rule brought the already tottering Moghul empire virtually to an end. The Europeans in India were quick to seize the opportunity offered by this decline, and the British and French soon became bitter rivals for power in India.

The 'East Indies' was a vague term covering the whole Far East. In fact, in terms of sheer profit the East India Company made more money out of China than it ever did out of India. However, India was the closer country and also offered better trading possibilities.

The first task the British faced was to break the Portuguese monopoly, which had been soundly established for a century. From their headquarters on the island of Goa, the Portuguese had built up a complete chain of factories and trading posts and they wanted no European rivals close by.

William Hawkins and Emperor Jahangir

It was 12,000 miles from England to India and the voyage took at least six months. Early British ships failed to find the way or foundered in storms. It was not until 1608 that the *Hector*, under Captain William Hawkins – a nephew of the Sir John Hawkins of the Spanish Main – became the first East India Company ship to reach India. They landed at Surat, 167 miles to the north of Bombay and right in the thick of the Portuguese-influenced territory.

At first, curious Indians followed them around in the streets, marvelling at the whiteness of their skins. The Indian traders welcomed them because they gave better prices than the Portuguese. Banquets were arranged and Hawkins was loaned a house to live in. Then the Portuguese, furious at this trespassing on their preserve, seized Hawkins's ship and demanded of the local Indian viceroy that he be arrested. However, Hawkins had brought with him a letter from King James I to the Moghul emperor in Delhi and, although the emperor's control over his sub-continent was less than fully effective, the viceroy was afraid to interfere with so important a state communication. Hawkins further assisted matters with bribes to the viceroy. The Portuguese tried to assassinate him but Hawkins obstructed them by persuading the viceroy to enforce a law forbidding the carrying of weapons in Surat. After five months a letter came from the emperor summoning Hawkins to court at Agra, 400 miles inland.

This was a considerable journey in itself and Hawkins decided to travel in style so as to make a good impression on his arrival. He hired fifty Pathan horsemen as his escort, as well as archers and musketeers, and it turned out that he needed them. The Portuguese had bribed minor princelings on the route to attack and kill him – there was one actual battle in which Hawkins's men defeated a rajah's private army.

The Moghul dynasty had originally been conquerors from Turkey and Hawkins knew Turkish, which meant that he could talk directly to the emperor. The court was one of breath-taking splendour. The Emperor Jahangir, with diamonds on his head and pearls the size of eggs on his chest, sat on his high throne surrounded by noblemen and attendants. The air was perfumed and the floor laid with thick carpets. Scribes recorded everything the emperor said and every action he took, even to his performing natural functions. When the emperor heard lawsuits and criminal charges, he had forty executioners, armed with axes, around the throne ready to inflict immediate punishment.

According to Hawkins, there were 12,000 elephants in the palace stables and 100 tame lions in the gardens. Jahangir, son of the much greater Akbar, was an impulsive man with a curiously mixed personality. He could be fiendishly cruel and he was a habitual drunkard. Yet he knew much about the world, was curious to learn more, and had excellent taste in artistic matters. He had a great collection of Chinese porcelain, which he loved. One day a piece of it got broken and the court comptroller, in a panic, sent off to China to fetch a replacement. But the journey to China and back took two years, and after only one year the

View of the Portuguese colony of Goa about 1635. Goa was the first territorial possession of the Portuguese in Asia, and became the capital of their eastern empire.

The emperor Jahangir with a portrait of his father, Akbar. In spite of strong opposition from the Portuguese, the emperor was persuaded by William Hawkins and Sir Thomas Roe to sanction English trade at Surat.

emperor suddenly demanded to see that particular piece. The comptroller confessed what had happened. His punishment, carried out on the spot, was to receive 120 lashes with the whip, to be cudgelled by twenty men and then to go to prison for the rest of his life. Later the emperor released him on condition that he travelled to China to find additions for the porcelain collection.

The imperial family and court were Moslem – the bulk of India had been ruled by Moslem conquerors for the past 400 years – but Jahangir was attempting a policy of conciliation with the subordinate Hindu rulers.

The Portuguese were ready for Hawkins's arrival and a Jesuit stationed himself by the throne to act as interpreter. When Hawkins presented his letter from James I, the Jesuit glanced at it and said it was worthless. Hawkins, to their surprise, then spoke directly to the emperor in Turkish: 'Your Majesty, how can this letter be ill-written when my King demands favour of your Majesty?' The emperor saw sense in this and said he would talk privately to Hawkins later on.

Hawkins must have been an amusing conversationalist, with stories of life in Europe and anecdotes about his travels, and very rapidly, it seems, he became close friends with the emperor. The two men sat up into the night carousing together and the emperor procured for Hawkins a Christian wife, an Armenian. Hawkins had the wedding ceremony performed by his English cook rather than let the Jesuits have any hand in it.

This very first relationship between a Moghul emperor and an agent of the East India Company set what eventually was to become the pattern for the future. The legal framework for the

A view of the British factory at Surat, on the banks of the Tappee. At the end of the sixteenth century the Portuguese were masters of the Surat seas, but in 1612 their naval supremacy was destroyed by the British, and Surat became the seat of a presidency under the East India Company.

company ultimately taking over India was that it acted theoretically as the emperor's agents. Not until 1857 was the Moghul regime formally abolished, although it had by then been long an empty shell. Hawkins's ambition, however, was not conquest but a licence to trade, and he cajoled the emperor into granting it. Immediately the Portuguese, whose fleet controlled the sea around India, set up a blockade which threatened to strangle all trade. The emperor, who had no navy of his own, was afraid of losing his customs revenues and so cancelled Hawkins's licence. Deeply disappointed, Hawkins sailed home to England and died during the voyage.

Prestige and profit

Before his death Hawkins wrote a report on conditions in India and so the next East India Company expedition, under Captain Thomas Best, came better prepared. Best, who arrived in 1611, realised he would have to defeat the Portuguese in a sea battle if he was ever to enhance his prospects. Soon after his arrival a Portuguese armada of more than twice his strength attacked his ships, but Best held his own, sinking one enemy vessel. The other attackers then withdrew, being short of water, and it looked as though they had been put to flight. Portuguese prestige tumbled sharply and the emperor, feeling that he was no longer dependent on them for his sea communications, gave Best a licence to trade and build factories. There were a few more armed clashes with the Portuguese but within five years the British were firmly established.

The first East India Company factories were at Masulipatam and Surat on the eastern coast. By 1641 they had moved around to the other side of the continent by founding Madras, and twenty years later, as part of the marriage contract between Charles II and his Portuguese queen, they acquired Bombay. (In fact Bombay remained British crown property but the company was allowed a lease of it.) In 1690 they founded what was to become the biggest British settlement of all, Calcutta.

It was a most lucrative trade. The East India Company became the richest and most influential commercial concern in London – in a single year it distributed £100,000 in bribes to check a proposal in parliament to break its monopoly. Individual traders, acting through the company or as illicit poachers upon its preserves, piled up what today would rank as multimillionaire fortunes. For the ambitious young man who wanted to make money, India was the obvious place. It was hard work, the climate was foul and the risk of fatal disease was high. But those who survived and had been skilful in their dealings were able to come home again in early middle age to retire in opulence.

The returned Indian 'nabobs', as they were nicknamed, were strange figures, with their rough manners, their Indian servants and their liking for highly spiced food. They would marry, buy country estates and perhaps purchase a 'rotten borough' and so a seat in parliament. They were too uncouth to win complete social success, although they tried hard to impress their neighbours by building splendid new houses – much of the lavish tradition of eighteenth century English country house architecture sprang from the 'nabobs'. Within a generation, however, their families were absorbed into the English upper classes. The Pitt family, which produced two eighteenth-century prime ministers, had its fortunes founded by a nabob.

The character of company operations – the Indians called it 'John Company' – had little in common with the stoical administration of India by an uncorrupt civil service in the Victorian period. Life for the British adventurer was short and so it had to be profitable. Bribery and fraud were commonplace – the only justification being that the British were no more unscrupulous than anybody else in their business methods. Away in India for twenty years or more, usually without ever returning home on leave, the company official in Surat, Madras or Bombay built up his own way of life.

He started as a clerk on a pittance of a salary and in his earlier years was supposed not to trade on his own account. The clerk, toiling on his high stool with a servant pulling a 'punkah' to provide some slight alleviation to the heat, led a miserable life. He was too poor to afford his own home, and so he lived in a company hostel where the discipline was something like that of a boarding school. The young Robert Clive – the man who won India for Britain – was so unhappy as a junior clerk that he attempted to shoot himself. Some of the juniors improved their way of life by borrowing from bazaar moneylenders at exorbitant rates of interest. This rapidly became a recognised custom, the moneylenders banking on the possibility that the penurious youth might eventually earn a fortune, but those who followed it usually found that they had missed the point of being in India. By the time they had paid off the moneylenders, they had no nabob's fortune left to bring back to England.

After from five to ten years service, the official received permission to trade on his own account. Every senior official of the company, even the chaplains, did this. Eventually the absurd position developed of the company making a loss on its operations in India and asking the British government for a subsidy while its own officials, using company facilities, made private fortunes. The successful trader came to live like a prince, setting up a household with a hundred servants. If he walked in the street he had a servant with him holding an umbrella over him to shield him from the sun. Usually, however, he did not walk at all but progressed in a palanquin, a kind of covered bed which took four servants to carry it plus a fifth to fan the occupant. His friends were Indian aristocrats, with whom he went tiger-shooting.

In this early period the British had little colour prejudice and mixed socially with Indians so far as Hindu caste requirements permitted. If it suited a trader's business purposes, he was willing to kow-tow to a native potentate as to a fellow white man. He often wore Indian clothes. At this time very few British women went out to India and sexual relationships between the British officials and Indian women were commonplace. Even marriages, in one form or another, were not unknown and up to the early eighteenth century did the British husband no social damage. However, the mistresses and wives, if they were caste Hindus, had polluted themselves and were driven out of their community. Their only resort, very often, was to turn Christian.

By the eighteenth century a distinct 'Eurasian' community had come into existence, the offspring of British fathers and Indian mothers. They kept their British surnames and Christian religion; used the English language, and for generations referred to the Britain they had never seen as 'home'. By the nineteenth century their community, which had become largely self-propagating, far out-numbered the pure-bred British in India, and they were looked down upon and even despised. The colour-conscious Victorians, in a circular argument, claimed that the Eurasians were despised because they had low status and had low status because they were despised. Eventually even the name 'Eurasian', which would seem to be a decent, logical one in its derivation, came to be something near a term of abuse, like that of 'nigger' applied to an African. It was replaced, for polite purposes, with 'Anglo-Indian' and even, eventually, 'Anglo-Pakistani'. However, in the early period of East India Company operations, the Eurasians suffered from no prejudice and were a useful auxiliary.

New towns

Around each company settlement grew a sizeable town. Madras, by the early eighteenth century, had a population of 250,000, and eventually Calcutta, which started as a few warehouses on the bank of the Hoogli river, became one of the world's greatest cities. The British proudly claimed that the people were attracted because the settlements were secure and well-governed. There may well have been some truth in this, but the more obvious explanation is that the people came for business reasons, direct and indirect.

To keep order in the settlements and to defend them, the company created its own private army. In the early period the soldiers were low-class European mercenaries of mixed nationality, a hundred or so of them in each settlement. Later the company raised Indian regiments under British officers. For a long time the company army was purely defensive in conception but, gradually, it came to be used in *ad hoc* alliances with Indian rulers at war with each other. The British were rewarded for their services with some new trading concession or monopoly, or with plain cash, and the Indians thought of them as just a useful ally.

For the first century and more, the British population in India was extremely small. When Madras had a population of 250,000 in 1740, the number of British was only about a

Part of a set of carved and painted chessmen, made about 1800,
representing members of the army of the East India Company.

Left: *East Indiamen off Deptford. The dockyard at Deptford was constructed in 1609 when the need for good ships for the East Indian trade had become urgent. The company's ships had to be prepared at any time to fight off the armed trading vessels of rival countries, and indeed, many such battles took place.*

Above: *this remarkable Moghul painting, dating from the end of the sixteenth century, demonstrates how rapidly European influences took root. Jesuit missionaries, who had been active in India since the time of St Francis Xavier, often circulated religious engravings, and the cosmopolitan interests of the emperors Akbar and Jahangir further encouraged the court artists to emulate European styles and subjects.*

Left: *the Taj Mahal, most splendid example of all Moghul architecture, was built by the Shah Jahan, the son of Jahangir, in 1629 as a tomb for his beloved wife. By Jahan's time the Moghul empire was already greatly weakened by internal squabbles and expensive wars of conquest.*

hundred. An Indian regiment of 1,000 men then had only three or four British officers. Against the vast Indian scene as a whole – it comprised one sixth of the human race – the British were only a peripheral factor. Mainstream Indian politics proceeded as if they were not there at all.

The Indian heritage

In many ways, the sub-continent of India was a contradiction, being both a united and a highly disunited country. Union came from the Hindu language and culture and from natural frontiers on all sides. Disunion came from its sheer size and from its division into countless different racial and caste groups. India had twelve major languages. For over 1,000 years she had been a prey to conquerors, the latest being the Turkish Moslems to whom the Moghul Empire belonged. In theory the Moghul writ ran through the whole of India except the extreme south but under him were multitudes of viceroys and semi-independent princes who struggled with each other to extend their wealth and power.

There was nearly always a civil war going on somewhere in India, just as, it might be remarked, there was nearly always a war going on somewhere in Europe. It was to become the fashion for such Indian nationalist politicians as Jawaharlal Nehru between the two world wars to claim that the British had deliberately fomented civil strife in order to advance their own power. This certainly did happen in one or two local instances, and for local reasons, but it was not true in general – most of the wars took place in regions remote from the British settlements.

The Moghul dominion over India lasted about twice as long as the British dominion, but by the end of the seventeenth century it was decaying. It was still producing masterpieces of art and architecture and, indeed, the imperial capitals at Agra and Delhi were the most splendid in the world. The emperor, Shah Jahan, was overcome with grief when his favourite wife, Mumtaz, died in giving birth to her fourteenth child by him, and he decided to give her the finest tomb that the world had ever seen.

Work on the tomb began in 1632 and took twenty two years to complete: semi-precious stones were inlaid according to methods which had been developed in Italy and white marble was carved, in Persian style, into shapes of supreme intricacy and beauty. The emperor was obsessed by its design and construction to such an extent that some thought he was mad. By the time it was finished he had been deposed and was living out the remainder of his life as a prisoner, devoting himself to religious exercises. But over his wife's tomb – the Taj Mahal – he had been completely successful. Beyond doubt, the Taj Mahal, especially when seen by moonlight, is the most beautiful tomb in the world, indeed many would maintain that it is the most beautiful building of any kind. In comparison, the British trading posts which were developing on the coast at the same time were insignificant.

By the end of the seventeenth century, five European countries – Britain, France, Portugal, the Netherland and Denmark – maintained trading posts in India, complete with small private armies for defensive purposes. The original monopoly holders, the Portuguese, continued to prosper but were making no new advances. The Dutch and the Danes operated on a relatively small scale. However both the French and the British were energetic in promoting their interests and they were bitter rivals. In the following century the French were the first to contemplate seeking major political power in India, partly with a view to ejecting the British. On their side, the British counterattacked.

As in America, so also in India, the British and the French had to fight it out for mastery.

44

The English Fort of Bombay

Above: *the English fort at Bombay. The territory was originally under Hindu rule, and was ceded to the Portuguese in 1534. The directors of the East India Company, who had for some time had their eye on Bombay, where they would have a large harbour as well as being free from Moghul control, were given their opportunity in 1665: the land was presented to the British as part of the dowry of the Infanta of Portugal on her marriage to Charles II.*

Masulipatam (now Masulipatnam) near Madras, one of the early trading stations of the East India Company. On the last day of the sixteenth century Queen Elizabeth I signed the royal charter for the company, which conferred the sole right of trading with the East Indies for a term of fifteen years. In 1609 James I renewed the charter 'for ever', although it could be revoked if trade were to prove unprofitable to the realm.

Rivalry with France

The British forces scaling the Heights of Abraham. Proof of Wolfe's unusual power of leadership was given by the success of the daring attack on Quebec. Having tricked his opponent General Montcalm into believing that his attack would be on the main front, Wolfe took a small force of men towards the cliff face at night in boats with muffled oars. In the small hours of the morning they scaled the cliffs, and advanced towards the city, taking the enemy completely by surprise.

For about eight centuries, until the Battle of Waterloo in 1815, there existed an hereditary feud between the British and the French. The two countries glowered at each other across the English Channel and thought it normal to be at war. It was like some ghastly blood sport, and which side, if either, eventually won is none too clear. Traditional-style British and French history books seem to be describing totally different events, so diverse are their accounts.

In the eighteenth century Britain and France were at war with each other more often than not. The causes were usually connected with European diplomacy and with attempts to promote the interests of particular candidates for particular European thrones. Whatever the cause of the war and whatever shape the shifting European alliances had taken, Britain and France were always on opposite sides. The effects of the wars—there were six of them during the century—made themselves felt in the settlements in America and India so that fighting broke out overseas as well. Generally the colonists were pleased about a war because it gave them an excuse to attack their local rivals. However, it was difficult to synchronise the overseas conflicts with what was going on in Europe. It took six months to send a letter to America and receive a reply and at least two years when writing to India. The colonial wars tended to start later than their European counterparts and to continue after the European fighting had finished; and the side which got the news first was at a considerable advantage.

France had the larger population, the more efficient government and the stronger army, indeed, she was reckoned to be the chief European power. Britain was becoming the richer and, on the whole, had the better navy. The song *Rule Britannia, Britannia rule the waves* was written by James Thomson in 1749, and the way in which it rapidly became a popular favourite illustrates the British urge to dominate the oceans. In all the six wars between Britain and France in the eighteenth century, colonial aspirations were part of the motivation on both sides. The French colonial effort tended to be the more centrally directed, either from Paris or by such energetic local officials as Dupleix in India. British expansionism, on the other hand, depended more on individuals, although the government was always willing to defend their revenues.

The struggle for America

At the time America seemed to be a much more significant theatre than India. In America daughter nations were being formed, redounding to the glory of the mother country. India was simply a place for profitable business, and political control was a matter of only negative significance. Most of the fighting took place in America. The French, at first, seemed to be the losers, but then the rules of the game changed and, by siding with the rebellious British colonists, France helped to break the major British power in North America.

France came very near to being the chief power in North America. In addition to Canada, where she had 'New France' settled by a complete colonial population, she also had Acadia (Nova Scotia) and the great territory of Louisiana which ran to the west of the British colonies. The French Americans were better than the British Americans at making friends with the native Indian tribes and used them as active allies. The British Americans considered this unfair, and were outraged when Indians, allied with the French, tortured and killed prisoners. That Indians did not obey the politer conventions of European warfare helped greatly to embitter the conflict. Both sides were aggressive. The British colonies, particularly Massachusetts, mounted private expeditions of their own against the French and sometimes received support from expeditions of regular military and naval forces sent by London. The surveyor and

Fires in New York during the advance of the British forces under Sir William Howe from Long Island to Manhattan. Howe defeated Washington's army and forced it to retreat across the Sound to Manhattan.

Lord Cornwallis surrenders to Washington at Yorktown in October 1781. The loss of Cornwallis's army marked, in effect, the end of the war; the following year Britain recognised American independence.

plantation owner George Washington gained his first fighting experience in such conflicts – it irked him that his American militia man's commission ranked him below all British officers with the king's commission.

The French, equally aggressive, constructed a chain of fortified posts which, if it had ever been fully completed, would have run all the way from Canada down to their city of New Orleans at the mouth of the Mississippi. Thus the British colonies would have been sealed permanently within the eastern seaboard, and the rest of the North American continent would have been open for French settlement. A point of particular conflict was the area of Lake Michigan where Chicago now stands. Pioneering British Americans, pushing out into the wilderness in search of new land, found themselves up against French outposts.

For the first half of the eighteenth century the fighting swayed backwards and forwards with no substantial result. The American colonists captured the French fortress of Louisburg on Breton Island, off the Canadian coast, but were furious when, in the next peace treaty, the British traded it back for Madras, which the French had captured in India. To the British this seemed to be a sensible deal, in the circumstances of the moment, but the Americans could not understand why they should sacrifice territory to suit British interests at the other side of the world. Florida and some of the smaller West Indian islands moved between British, French and Spanish control according to particular military successes and diplomatic negitiations.

The tide turns

The British and the colonists made their major break-through, during the Seven Years War of 1756 to 1763, which was nominally caused by a dispute in Central Europe about the Prussian occupation of Silesia. Britain and Prussia were allies together against the rest of Europe, and for a long time it looked as if they would be defeated. But Prussia had a leader of genius in Frederick the Great, whose dynasty was eventually to unite Germany, and Britain threw up one of her greatest prime ministers, William Pitt the Elder. Pitt kept his eye as firmly upon America as he did upon Europe. He was the first British prime minister to act specifically as a national leader. Compared with him, the monarch, George II, was a shadow. When the king, encouraged by a group of politicians, dismissed Pitt from office, there was a public outcry and demands that he be re-instated. Towns and cities from all over Britain expressed their admiration for him by sending a 'shower of golden boxes' containing documents making him an honorary freeman. This was an imperialist as well as a nationalist mood, with the general public, or the articulate sections of it, anxious to win new territories overseas.

Plagued with gout and often afflicted with moods of deep melancholy during which he sat silent and still for hours, his head in his hands, Pitt nevertheless was an inspiring leader and a brilliant public speaker. The unreformed House of Commons was a corrupt body. About half its membership sat for 'rotten boroughs', where election contests were settled by bribery of a handful of electors, or for 'pocket boroughs' which were virtually owned outright. Pitt himself owned Old Sarum, which had only six voters; his grandfather had bought it on returning from India with a fortune. Thus Pitt had no formal control over the House of Commons, the majority of its members being under the patronage of a caucus led by the Duke of Newcastle. But by oratory and force of personality Pitt could dominate the sessions of the House. It was said that one glare from his eyes was enough to frighten off a member from making a speech attacking him. Similarly in private, Pitt had the gift of making everyone who came to see him feel inspired and capable of great things. To run the war, he set up an office with six secretaries – whom he never

allowed to sit in his presence – and his power stretched right across the globe.

Pitt had a special genius for finding talented young men, one of whom was James Wolfe, a regimental commander and acting brigadier, aged only thirty-two. This sickly, intellectual man who combined a love of poetry with a scientific study of war, nevertheless worshipped efficiency and had a brilliant mind. In 1759, to the consternation of the army, Pitt promoted him to the rank of major-general in command of the military side of a joint army-navy expedition against Quebec. In any period, thirty-two would count as an unusually young age for a general but in the eighteenth century, hidebound by seniority, it was regarded as actually shocking. Admirals in the British navy at that time were appointed entirely on seniority, it taking at least twenty years on the captains' list to get to the top and thus obtain the next vacancy for rear-admiral. Wolfe's opponent in Quebec, the French Marquis of Montcalm, was fifteen years his senior.

The fall of Quebec

Montcalm was a serious opponent. Early in the war he drove deep into British territory and captured what is now Albany, the capital of New York State; he was only 140 miles from New York city itself, and the sea. Now he was established back in Quebec, awaiting the arrival of supplies and reinforcements from France – these were being hindered by the naval blockade Pitt had inaugurated. Montcalm believed Quebec to be impregnable. The first line of defence was the St Lawrence river itself, which was regarded as unnavigable by a major fleet which was unfamiliar with it. The British expedition was expected to founder, or turn back, long before it reached the city. However, the British naval commander, Saunders, and his captains were excellent seamen and they conveyed Wolfe and his army to within four miles of Quebec.

Montcalm had drawn up his army along a six-mile ridge which was the only obvious approach to the city. Frontal attack up the ridge was likely to be disastrous to anybody who tried it. Other approaches were protected by sheer cliffs which, Montcalm said, could be held by a hundred men against an entire army. It looked like a stalemate, with the danger of Wolfe's army being destroyed by the Canadian winter if it waited too long. For two months both sides skirmished while Wolfe, wretchedly ill with rheumatism and gravel, tried to work out a plan. Eventually he decided upon the colossal gamble of attempting to scale the cliffs in a surprise night attack – reconnaissance had revealed a zig-zag path running sketchily up the cliff face.

To carry out this plan at all, with the rather stiff and parade ground character of the British army, required unusual leadership. This Wolfe was able to exert. He had the love and support of his men – the whole army grieved when he fell ill in his tent. It also required the element of complete surprise; the French advanced posts must be passed without their knowing what was happening. Accordingly Wolfe started great activity on the main front, against Montcalm's army on the ridge, as if he were going to back everything on frontal assault. Then at night, in a procession of boats rowed with muffled oars, he took 1,600 men towards the cliff face. He is supposed to have whispered Gray's *Elegy* on the way and to have remarked that he would rather have written that than take Quebec. When a French sentry challenged the boats, a Highland officer with a good French accent replied that they were a supply convoy, and this was believed.

In the small hours of the morning, Wolfe's force climbed the cliff and reached the Heights of Abraham above. Wolfe changed into a fresh new uniform and advanced towards the city, at first meeting almost no opposition. By the time Montcalm had learned of the landing and remarshalled his army, the British

William Pitt, 1st Earl of Chatham. When Pitt joined the ministry in 1756 as secretary of state, the government had already been trying unsuccessfully for two years to deal with fighting between France and England in the colonies. In 1756 England formally declared war. Though handicapped by the loathing of George II, who called him 'devil incarnate', Pitt managed by his energy, skill, and flair for picking the right men, to win a major European war which firmly established Great Britain as an imperial power.

James Wolfe was thirty-two when he was chosen by Pitt to command the military side of the joint army-navy expedition against Quebec. In spite of the dismay of the army at the appointment of such a young man, General Wolfe proved an excellent choice; although introverted, intellectual and frequently ill, he had a passion for efficiency and a brilliant mind, and was sincerely loved by his men.

were ashore in full strength and then the parade ground qualities of their army were supreme. Six British battalions marched forward. When they fired, it was said, the sound was like that of six gigantic shots from one gun. The French, who were mostly colonial irregulars unaccustomed to formal battle, broke and scattered. At the moment of victory both Wolfe and his opponent, Montcalm, fell mortally wounded. For years afterwards, his mother, a widow, had to quarrel with the war department about whether she was entitled to a colonel's or a major-general's pension.

British North America

The fall of Quebec represented, in effect, the fall of French North America. The following year the British took Montreal against relatively slight opposition and in the peace treaty in 1763 France formally ceded Canada to Great Britain, plus what is now the state of Mississippi from Louisiana. As a side arrangement in the general sorting out of territories she ceded the rest of Louisiana to Spain. Later France had Louisiana back again and for a moment Napoleon Bonaparte, as First Consul of the Republic, thought of reviving old dreams and using it as the basis for a new French American empire. Had Napoleon indeed gone to America the course of history might have been substantially changed. However, on second thoughts he dropped the idea and sold the territory to the United States for £3 million.

In 1763 the British appeared to be supreme in North America, but there were different ideas of what, precisely, this implied. The British thought of it being a section of the whole British Empire—that term was just coming into use—and that the colonists ought to be proud to belong to so powerful an organisation. The colonists themselves took a more parochial view. Although they could not claim to have beaten the French on their own, they had contributed some forces towards what they considered was their war, fought in their own interests. Few people, if any, drew the direct conclusions at that moment, but obviously future British military help was superfluous and the colonists could afford to go ahead on their own.

The thirteen British colonies which formed the original United States of America had a population of three million white men and about three quarters of a million Negro slaves. They were, therefore, a sizeable population by the standards of the time—the British population at home was only about eight million and Britain was a world power. In ancestry the colonists were overwhelmingly British, the only significant exception being about 150,000 Germans, mostly in Pennsylvania. Of the thirteen, twelve had been founded in the seventeenth century and one, Georgia, in the eighteenth century. Thus they mostly had a settled political tradition extending back several generations. The methods of government varied. In some the colonial governors were appointed by the British crown, in some by 'proprietors' and in two, Connecticut and Rhode Island, they were elected. Every colony had an elected legislature. To the British these legislatures had no more status than a municipal council but the colonists were coming to regard them as equivalents to parliament at Westminster.

On the whole it was a prosperous society, based upon individualism and private enterprise. Its basis was still agriculture, with pioneers going out into the wilderness to establish new farms. Some of these 'backwoods' families lived for months, or even years, without receiving visitors and they became uncouth and strange, the men overgrown with hair, the women in tatters. Hunting for furs was central to the economy, since there was an enormous demand in Europe for beaver hats. Then there were the merchants, who usually ran small family businesses, and dominated the cities—such places as New York and Boston had grown into considerable cities even by European standards.

Agriculture and Slavery

A specialist form of agriculture which was of relatively recent growth and of increasing importance was that of the large-scale plantation based upon slave labour. Originally it had been copied from the sugar plantations and many found it a sure way to wealth. Plantation crops, notably cotton, required an extensive acreage and a large labour force from which hard, repetitive work was required rather than skill. Profits could run at forty per cent on capital a year and from the proceeds the planters built splendid homes on the British rural magnate model, with marble imported from Europe. Their mass production of cotton lowered prices and so, they could and did hold, they were benefactors of the poor in Europe.

Plantation agriculture made slavery for the first time a major force in British North America. In the eighteenth century the slave trade reached to enormous proportions. It has been computed that, at the peak, 100,000 Africans every year were being torn from their homes for slavery in the Americas. The plantation slaves, at least, led the most miserable lives. Their owners were half-afraid of them—a single family might own 5,000 slaves—and determined to exploit them to the limit. They worked in the fields under the whip and a slave's only hope of a step up in the world was to be promoted to wield the whip over his fellows. A plantation slave was not allowed to marry or to have a normal family; his children were the property of his

owner who could, and did, sell them as he pleased. Seldom had exploitation of human beings been more ruthless.

The development of the plantations in the eighteenth century took place under British law; indeed the American ones were based on the model of those in the British West Indies. Slavery even existed in Great Britain itself—some 14,000 African slaves were being used as domestic servants and regarded as their masters' property. Their average value was about £40 each—say £500 in modern values, or the price of a small car. However, in 1772 a test case was brought in the court of King's Bench in London over a Negro called James Somersett who had been brought to England as a slave and then turned destitute into the streets by his master. Later the master had attempted to reclaim him and had seized him by force.

The Lord Chief Justice, Lord Mansfield, was none too eager to hear the case. He believed that it was the primary function of the law to protect property, but knew that he would have to give a ruling destroying property worth £500,000. He would have preferred the slavery position to remain in ambiguity and tried to persuade the parties to the dispute to settle out of court by mutual agreement. Eventually, however, he had to give judgment and to rule that 'the state of slavery was so odious that nothing can be suffered to support it but positive law'; since there was no positive British law on the subject, the slaves had to be freed. Disgusted at the loss of their property, many of the

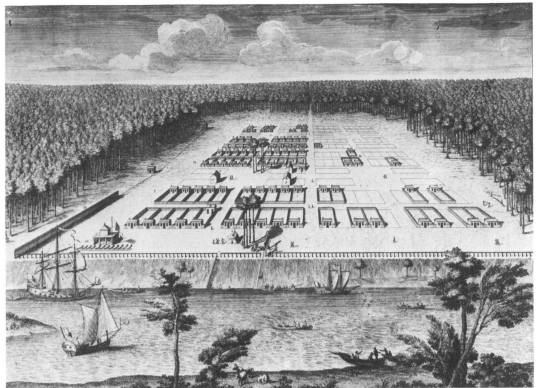

The death of Wolfe. Quebec
surrendered on 18 September, after
six days of open battle on the
Plains of Abraham. Neither
Montcalm nor Wolfe were
present at the end—both were killed
in the battle, but Wolfe's last
sight as he lay mortally wounded
was of the enemy running in
confusion, and his last words
were: 'Now God be praised, I
will die in peace'.

Above: this view of Savannah,
Georgia, as it stood in 1734, was
dedicated to the Trustees. Georgia
was the last founded of the
Thirteen Colonies. England
wished to establish a buffer colony
to protect South Carolina from
Spanish invasion, and the
philanthropist James Oglethorpe
wanted to create a refuge for
English debtors. He obtained a
charter from George II in 1732,
and a board of trustees was
appointed to administer the
territory.

Colonial Williamsburg. The Old
Court House. Williamsburg
became the capital of Virginia in
1699, and was the scene of
important conventions during the
independence movement.
Restoration and reconstruction of
its many fine eighteenth-century
buildings was begun in 1929.

masters just threw their slaves out with no money and no means of earning any. For thousands of the ex-slaves their last state was worse than their first but charitable donations enabled them to be shipped off to Sierra Leone, West Africa, which had been acquired for their intended benefit.

There was no attempt to extend the Mansfield ruling to the colonies but, the plantations apart, slavery showed some disposition to die out of its own accord. Thus in the 1770s the sewage disposal system of the city of New York was gangs of slaves, with buckets on their heads, who carried all the sewage to the Hudson River. But as soon as pipes and drains had been laid, they became superfluous. For any job requiring even the slightest degree of skill or enthusiasm, free labour was infinitely the more efficient. It was the special demands of the southern plantations, with their huge profits, that protracted slavery as a major force into the nineteenth century.

The British parliament, under humanitarian pressure, legislated first to make conditions in slave ships more comfortable and then, in 1807, to abolish the slave trade altogether. About a sixth of the strength of the Royal Navy was then employed on anti-slavery control off the African coast; it arrested slave ships of every nationality, the naval crew receiving a bounty of £5 a head for every slave they liberated. However, ships under the United States flag resisted the British claim to a right to search them for slaves, and although the trans-Atlantic trade was now illegal, slavery as such still continued in British colonies. It was particularly vigorous in the plantations of the West Indies, and it was not until 1833–only thirty years before American emancipation–that it was finally abolished in the British Empire.

The plantation owners in the American south formed a kind of landed aristocracy, the archetypal representative, in American folklore, being George Washington. In plantations around his elegant Virginia home, called Mount Vernon after the British Admiral Vernon under whom he had served in the West Indies, Washington maintained a labour force of about 2,000 slaves. He treated them with reasonable humanity, much as he might have treated a stable of valuable horses, and thought that, in theory, slavery could not be expected to last for ever. However for the meantime he bought and sold slaves and had them whipped whenever they displeased him. Another slave-owning Virginian of a similar type was Thomas Jefferson, who was to write most of the American Declaration of Independence.

It was an alliance of southern planters with sharp-witted businessmen, lawyers, and intellectuals from the north which produced the American Revolution and with it the apparent destruction of the British Empire. Disruption was inevitable.

Trade

The British thought that the principal function of colonies was to serve the interests of the mother country and, indeed, there could be no other purpose in setting them up. They had to be subordinate. The colonists received as their reward the military security the mother country provided and trading advantages. The Americans, on the other side, thought they had the right to run their own affairs as they wished. In practice they thought of themselves less as 'Americans' than as members of a particular colony–Virginians, New Yorkers, New Englanders and so on. Even when president of the United States, Washington still regarded himself primarily as a Virginian.

The system had worked hitherto partly through inertia and partly because the external menace of the French bound the two sides together. The British parliament had imposed restrictions on the development of industry in the colonies, the idea being that it was the function of the colonies to provide raw materials only and to be a market for British manufacturers. Also a system

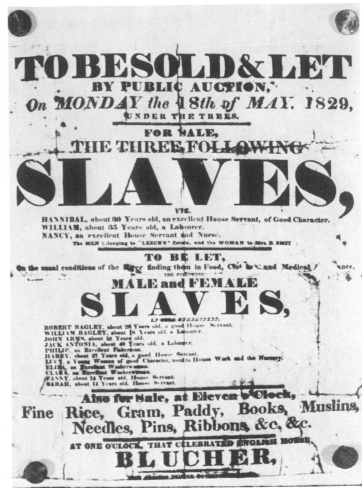

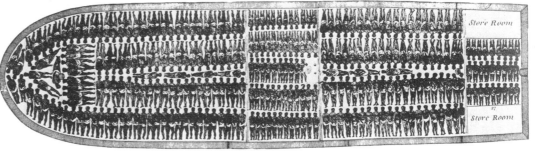

Top left: *a slave market in Virginia. In the seventeenth and eighteenth centuries large-scale plantations—mainly cotton and tobacco—became a sure way to wealth for the owners, and made slavery a major force in British North America. The plantation slaves led miserable lives; they worked hours which today seem unbelievable; they were allowed no normal family lives, and their children automatically became the property of the owner.*

Left: *slave labour on a tobacco plantation.*

Above: *the African slave trade flourished for some three centuries before its abolition in the early years of the nineteenth century. This plan shows the appalling conditions under which the slaves crossed the Atlantic.*

Left: *cartoon: 'The Bostonians Paying the Excise-Man, or Tarring and Feathering'. The crippling taxes imposed by the British government in an attempt to raise money to pay for the recent war incensed the American colonists; riots soon broke out and those in favour of separation became vocal and even violent. Tarring and feathering was a popular punishment for those who did not support the patriot cause. The cartoon was occasioned by the Boston Port Bill, which closed the port of Boston after the 'Tea Party', and precipitated formal revolt.*

Right: *the first important engagement in the War of Independence was at Bunker Hill in 1775, when British troops dislodged a patriot army which had occupied a strong position on a hill overlooking Boston.*

George III. It has been said that George lost America while in a fit of insanity, but recent research indicates that he was probably not insane at all. He obviously did not understand the issues over which the War of Independence was fought, and believed that the administration of his government suited the best interests of Americans.

of customs duties, administered by London-appointed officials, had been introduced to keep colonial trade on lines that suited the British. In practice these potentially burdensome restrictions had been ignored and the British had taken no trouble to enforce them. Some ninety per cent of the trade in dutiable goods was carried on by smuggling. The American customs cost more to administer than they produced in revenue – some of the officials actually lived in England and delegated their function in the vaguest way to 'deputies' on the spot.

The colonies revolt

With the victory over France, the British felt it was time to tighten up the American administration and to rationalise it. The war in America had cost the British £3 million and they could see no reason why the Americans should not contribute towards it. The customs collection was tightened up and the chancellor of the exchequer, Lord William Grenville, apparently on his own initiative and without consulting the rest of the cabinet, persuaded parliament to introduce an American stamp duty – a tax on all legal documents. Designed to raise £100,000 a year, the Stamp Act of 1764 attracted only a minimum of notice or debate in London, but it caused immediate uproar in America. To the ordinary dislike of paying taxes could be added the principle 'no taxation without representation'. The act was met with widespread boycotts and the American courts acquitted the offenders. The British quickly withdrew the act but this solved nothing as they continued to insist, in principle, on their right to tax the colonies. Thus began a chain of events which led to the American Declaration of Independence in 1776, and British recognition of it seven years later.

So far as any assessment is possible it can be reckoned that about a third of the colonists inclined towards 'loyalism' to the British connection, a third did not care at all and a third were in favour of separation. The 'loyalists' had virtually no organisation at all but the 'patriots' were vigorous and sometimes violent. Tarring and feathering was one remedy for people who

refused to support the 'patriot' cause. Step by step the 'patriots' advanced their organisation until they had inaugurated the 'Continental Congress', which met in Philadelphia as the first body representing all the colonies.

The original aim of the 'Continental Congress' was not independence but merely an equal negotiation with Britain to establish American 'rights'. Washington, who was one of the Virginian representatives in the congress, worked out a scheme by which the crown would have remained as a common link between Britain and the colonies; it was close to the later conception of 'dominion status'. Even after fighting had started, the colonists incorporated the British union jack in their flag and claimed that they were resisting a particular British government rather than Britain or the crown as a whole.

The London government under Lord North, with King George III playing a prominent role, was not quite so stupid as has been sometimes made out. George was later confined as a 'lunatic' and it has been held that he lost America while in a fit of insanity. In fact recent research has indicated that he was probably never mentally ill at all and certainly his actions and letters at the time of the American crisis show no mental un-balance. While George had little or no understanding of the motivation of the American patriots, he was actuated by the perfectly respectable aim of maintaining his crown and the British Empire. He honestly believed that the British Empire, as administered by his government, suited the best interests of the Americans themselves.

Both sides in the struggle were less than competent, and fighting broke out at Bunker Hill, Boston, in 1775, when British troops dislodged a patriot army which had occupied a strong point overlooking the city. The British won the battle, but their casualties were so severe that it was clear that they were facing formidable opposition. The following year the Congress declared American independence—twelve colonies voted in favour and New York abstained—and appointed George Washington as commander-in-chief of its army.

The War of Independence

Washington was six feet three inches tall, an exceptional height for the period. In any group in which he stood, he seemed to be head and shoulders above everyone else. Himself a gentlemanly and cultivated man, he was at pains to see that only 'gentlemen' were commissioned as officers and he employed flogging on a generous scale to keep the patriotic rank and file in order. He himself insisted that on serving with pay. His temperament was conservative and it was only later, and with some reluctance, that he accepted the aim of total independence.

Popular writing in America later made him into an un-believably glamorous figure, noble in his behaviour and a genius in his military and political leadership. In fact Washington was nothing of the kind—such stories as his confessing, when a child, to cutting down a cherry tree rather than tell a lie are total fiction; he was a slow-thinking Virginian squire whose main virtue was obstinacy. His generalship was at best indifferent and at worst plain bad. But against enormous difficulties presented by shortage of recruits and equipment, quarrels between the different colonies and lack of communications, he kept his army in existence. In the winter of 1778, quartered at Valley Forge, Pennsylvania, it nearly dissolved altogether through cold and starvation. The Pennsylvanian farmers preferred to sell their produce to the British occupying Philadelphia rather than to Washington's army. This was not so much because they were pro-British as because the British paid in pounds sterling where-as Washington only had paper dollars, issued by Congress, which were almost valueless. That Washington held together his army at Valley Forge was the major achievement of his life. The strength of his army varied from 40,000 down to 15,000, while British forces reached a maximum of 40,000.

The British could have won very easily by blockading the American coastline: the colonists depended upon imports from Europe for many of the necessities of life, including cloth and even salt, while the ammunition for Washington's army also had to come from Europe. Within two or three years the

Americans, who had virtually no fleet, would have been strangled, and forced to come to terms. The reason the British did not do this was that they did not consider themselves at war with the colonies as such, but only with particular rebels within them. Once the rebels had been eliminated, they believed that things would return to normal. To blockade the coast would be to admit that the rebels were in control.

The war was a protracted, desultory one lasting eight years. The British, formally, had the whip hand. For most of the time they occupied most of the cities – New York, Philadelphia, Charleston and Savannah. They were on reasonably good terms with the local population; in Philadelphia the wealthy classes arranged balls and parties for the British officers. However, they made the psychologically disastrous mistake of recruiting German mercenary regiments to add to their strength. George III, himself German by immediate descent and accustomed to spending several weeks a year in his principality of Hanover, was incapable of seeing what the reaction would be: German soldiers, to him, were the same as British ones. The Americans, however, in their trans-Atlantic isolation, had a much narrower outlook. To them it looked as if the man who claimed to be their king was hiring 'foreigners' to act as his butchers. The unpopularity of the German mercenaries did much to weaken the loyalist cause in America.

Naturally France, which had just lost its American territories, watched with the keenest interest. From the start she sent money and supplies to the American patriots. Benjamin Franklin, the journalist-scientist, who had been sent to argue the American cause at the bar of the British House of Commons, was despatched as the American agent in Paris. He urged the French to join the war on the rebels' side and, naturally, he attracted interest. The French had lost North America – why should the British not lose it too? It was almost unnatural for the British to be at war without France on the other side.

The decisive event of the war was the surrender at Saratoga in 1777 of the British General John Burgoyne, with 5,000 men. Burgoyne had been attempting to invade New England from Canada but the force that was supposed to link up with him from New York, to make a pincer movement, had instead gone off to capture Philadelphia. Burgoyne met the American General Horatio Gates, who had been sent by Washington with 18,000 men to obstruct him and, being vastly outnumbered, he surrendered. Burgoyne's capitulation so impressed the French with the possibility of Britain being defeated that they entered the war forthwith. Later the Netherlands and Spain also declared war on the Americans' side, which left Britain with no allies at all.

For a time the French navy seriously threatened British mastery of the Atlantic and smashed supply convoys. There was even a Franco-Spanish plan to invade Britain. Not until 1781, in the Battle of the Saints in the West Indies, did Admiral George Rodney rout the French and re-establish British maritime supremacy.

On the American mainland, despite the arrival of a professional French army, the fighting dragged on for years with no conclusive result. Washington's men, paid in worthless paper dollars and kept on for more than the three years for which they were originally engaged, reached the point of mutiny. At the beginning of 1781 three American regiments at New Jersey defied their officers and began to march off to the local legislature to present their grievances. Washington acted swiftly and savagely. He sent reliable forces after them, picked out a man from each mutinous regiment and forced his comrades to shoot him (one, in fact, was reprieved at the last moment). Soon afterwards, twelve mutineers were shot in Pennsylvania. Washington certainly recognised the dangerous state of his army.

Surrender at Yorktown

The French were ready to give up, or, rather, ready to settle for a compromise peace which would have allowed the colonists independence in only the narrowest strip of land on the eastern American coast. Had they been so restricted, they might never have spread across the continent to form the modern United States. Then, however, the British general Lord Cornwallis, one of the stupidest figures in the whole war, managed to trap himself and his army in the peninsula of Yorktown, Virginia. He was supposed to be assaulting South Carolina, and it has never been fully clear what he was doing in Yorktown. It could be that he was hoping for reinforcements by sea but, in fact, the French fleet arrived first and bombarded him. Combined American-French forces attacked from the land and, outnumbered four to one, Cornwallis surrendered.

The loss of Cornwallis's army marked, effectively, the defeat of Great Britain and the end of the war. The following year, the British recognised American independence on boundaries extending at least 1,200 miles westwards from the sea. Moreover the British failed to make any adequate provision for such loyalists or 'Tories' as had actively assisted them and now faced reprisals. Some 50,000 of them had to migrate hurriedly, and with a loss of their possessions, to form the beginnings of a substantial British settlement in Canada.

In 1783, the British finally evacuated New York. Washington went on to become the first president of the United States of America. Some called him 'His Majesty the President'; he himself had a leaning towards 'His Mightiness', as sounding less royal. Before long, however, the republican purists had their way and he became simply 'Mr President, sir'.

New horizons

It is perfectly plain in retrospect that the two countries had to part. They had different interests. Had the British managed to smash the 'patriot' movement of the 1770s it undoubtedly would have arisen again in the next generation, and would have gone on arising until it won. The Americans, with a continent to develop, were not going to be junior partners of the British. Similarly the British, with an empire to win, could never have allowed their policy to be swayed by the Americans. Any unity which could have been preserved would have been purely formal, and neither side would have been willing to give way to the other on anything important. In practice some degree of unity continued to exist. The British (including the Irish) continued to be by far the biggest suppliers of immigrants to the United States, and the British navy underwrote the American 'Monroe Doctrine' which forbade the future colonisation of any part of the American continents by a European power.

In some sense it can be held that the British expansionist and imperialist fell into schism at American independence. One stream, the Americans, considered it their 'manifest destiny' to advance, by purchase and settlement, right across the continent to the far west coast and so, ultimately, to make their country the richest in the world. The other stream, the British, went on to create the new British Empire which, for a time, was the most extensive power in the world. Both streams were the heirs of Drake and Raleigh.

At almost the same moment as they were losing the American colonies, the British were creating a new empire. The migration of the American 'loyalists' created Canada as a properly British dominion. The voyages of Cook opened up Australia and New Zealand for British settlement. The Napoleonic wars were to give the British the opportunity for winning yet more territory, including what is now South Africa. Above all the British were acquiring control of what was to be the brightest jewel of their empire in its classical form – India.

George Washington, the Virginia squire who was appointed by Congress as the Commander-in-Chief of the army of independence. He succeeded in keeping his army intact in the face of apparently insuperable odds.

George Washington and his men at Valley Forge, Pennsylvania, during the winter of 1778. Washington coped with enormous difficulties during this winter: there was a desperate shortage of food, recruits and equipment, quarrels were frequent and communications poor, but he managed to keep the army in existence.

Hessian troops recruited by the British Crown embark for the American colonies. The British made a fatal mistake in recruiting German mercenaries – to the Americans still loyal to the Crown it looked as though the king was hiring foreigners to do his dirty work. George III, himself of German descent, naturally could see nothing wrong in the decision, but it undoubtedly served to weaken the loyalist cause.

The Declaration of Independence, drafted in 1776, with Thomas Jefferson as its principal author, was recognised by Great Britain seven years later.

The hostage sons of Tipu Sultan delivering the treaty to Lord Cornwallis. Cornwallis was the first governor-general under the new Pitt legislation, which ruled that the governor was appointed by, and responsible to, the British government. During his years of rule a serious threat was posed by Tipu Sultan, the ruler of Mysore, who was greedy for more territory in southern India. Cornwallis, forced into action, defeated him at Seringapatam in 1792, forcing him to surrender half his dominions.

Brightest jewel of Empire

The world-wide rivalry between British and French was as strong in India as in America. Indeed, the administrations in London and Paris saw both countries as theatres of struggle in the same conflict for world power.

The French were the first to see India as a potential empire for themselves as well as a trading area. This was largely through the energy of Joseph Dupleix, who in 1742 became governor-general of French India (the British at that time had no governor-general but merely separate heads for their main trading posts at Calcutta, Bombay and Madras). Dupleix was a short energetic man, married to equally energetic half-Indian wife who set up a spy service to obtain information about the British. She was a fascinating woman who combined feminine charm with a toughness that enabled her to walk on the ramparts, under fire, to spur on the French soldiers during a siege.

Dupleix's territory, to start with, consisted mainly of the great French trading settlement of Pondicherry, on the east coast eighty-five miles south of Madras. Pondicherry was actually to remain French until 1956 when, finally, it was handed over to the Republic of India. Dupleix had the foresight to perceive that the administrative structure of the Moghul Empire was crumbling and that by skilful alliances and intrigue the French could extend their political power and so make their trade safer. In addition, Dupleix had a love of power for its own sake. The British obviously had to be eliminated from the sub-continent for his plans to succeed.

Before the arrival of Dupleix, the French and the British in India had not bothered to fight each other when their mother countries in Europe had gone to war. Dupleix changed that. A European war would give him the excuse to attack the British in India and so he eagerly awaited one. Meanwhile he set himself up in princely splendour at Pondicherry, using the title of 'Nawab' he obtained from the emperor, and formed alliances with Indian rulers and claimants to Indian thrones. When, in 1740, the War of the Austrian Succession started, with Britain and France on opposite sides, Dupleix attacked in India and captured Madras. To his disgust, however, the Paris government handed back Madras to the British in return for Louisbourg in the peace treaty of 1748 in Canada.

The next stage of the fighting, from 1750 to 1754, was unofficial in that Britain and France were not at war in Europe. Really it was an Indian civil war, with the British and French backing opposite sides. Dupleix's aim was to build up the power of the Nizam of Hyderabad, who was fighting to free himself from the suzerainty of the Nawab of the Carnatic. The British, fearful of the French becoming too powerful through their friendship with a victorious Nizam, allied themselves with the Nawab.

During this war there came to the fore the strange figure of Robert Clive, the true founder of the British Empire in India.

Clive of India

Proud, psychotic and highly intelligent, Clive might in some circumstances have become a master-criminal. He did become an opium addict. As a boy he had organised a gang of his fellows to extort 'protection money' from the shopkeepers in his home town of Market Drayton, Shropshire. He was expelled from school after school for misconduct, until when he was sixteen his father, a lawyer, packed him off to be an East India Company clerk in Madras. Clive continued to be quarrelsome and obstinate, seeking duels as solutions for disagreements. He quarrelled with his immediate superior in the office and the governor ordered him to apologise. Clive did so and the superior, anxious to make peace, invited Clive to dinner. 'No sir,' said Clive, 'the governor commanded me to apologise, but he did not command me to dine with you.'

Joseph Dupleix became Governor-General of French India in 1742, and set himself up in princely splendour at Pondicherry. His initially successful attempts to take over the reins of power from the weak Moghul emperors brought him into conflict with the British.

The wars gave Clive the opportunity to leave his clerk's stool and enter the career where his genius lay, that of a military commander. He was brave, inspiring and unscrupulous, and also extremely lucky. On at least three occasions he missed death by what seemed to be miracles. After distinguishing himself in minor battles, he set off, at the age of twenty-six, with the rank of captain and with a force of 500 mixed Indians and British to capture the key city of Arcot, capital of the Carnatic. He seized the city without trouble, its much superior garrison running away at his approach. Then combined French and Indian forces, whose strength was put at 10,000, counter-attacked, and Clive held out through a seven week siege. Food ran short and his Indian troops, so it was said, offered to let the white soldiers have all the rice while they themselves subsisted on the water in which the rice had been boiled. The besiegers also ran short of supplies and, after a final assault which Clive repelled, they withdrew.

The battle of Arcot, which Clive followed up with further successes, marked the end of French power in India. Dupleix, who had proclaimed himself 'Viceroy to the Emperor' in southern India, was finished. Not only had he failed to acquire political power but he had also reduced French trading profits in the attempt. He was recalled to France where he died, nine years later, broken and in poverty.

Clive, now aged twenty-eight, also returned home, but as a national hero. Although he could not have had much time for any serious trading, somehow he had acquired a fortune of £50,000, the equivalent of at least £500,000 today. Some of it he invested in India and the rest he converted into diamonds which he brought home with him. He was fêted as 'General' Clive and made friends with such rising young men as Lord Sandwich and the future Lord Mansfield. He lavished his money on gifts to his family, who were astonished that he had ever made good, and on a mansion in the West End of London. However he was so arrogant and ostentatious that, like other *nouveaux riches* nabobs, he failed really to fit in with London society. He bought himself a seat in the House of Commons but, to his fury, was ejected on an election petition. He had spent all his money and the day after he lost his seat he signed an agreement with the East India Company to return to India as a lieutenant-colonel on £70 a year.

The Black Hole of Calcutta

The decisive step towards British control of India came when the Nawab of Bengal, a youth only in his 'teens, decided to take over the British settlement of Calcutta, which was his property leased to the British. At the time the British were fortifying Calcutta against a possible French attack. The Nawab claimed – whether he was right or not is impossible to establish – that the Calcutta fortifications were really aimed against him and that the British were planning to overthrow him and replace him with their own candidate for the throne. He marched into Calcutta, without meeting resistance, and set about destroying British property. The British prisoners he seized – 145 men and one woman – were put for the night into a single cell measuring about eighteen feet square, with two small, barred windows.

This was the Black Hole of Calcutta, the most famous atrocity in British imperial history. Generation after generation of the British cherished the tradition of the Black Hole as showing how cruel Indians could be if allowed their heads. The very words passed into the language as a common simile for any crowded conditions – 'as bad as the Black Hole of Calcutta'.

In fact the Black Hole was the ordinary British prison in Calcutta, although the British probably never used it or intended to use it for more than a dozen or so prisoners at a time. The Nawab's guards, knowing that it was the ordinary prison, just pushed their British prisoners into it. They were pleased rather than otherwise that the British were to have an uncomfortable night.

It was an exceptionally hot night, the monsoon being overdue. It became the hotter, it was said, because the Nawab's armies were burning the British factories nearby. The 146 prisoners, pushed into the Black Hole, were so hot and short of air that they stripped off their clothes and tried to struggle towards the windows. The stench must have been appalling. Through the windows the prisoners offered bribes to the guards to transfer some of them to another room but the guards said they could not be moved without the consent of the Nawab, who could not be disturbed from his sleep. One guard put some water through a window and the prisoners trampled over each other to get it. As the night wore on, the prisoners began to die of sheer asphyxiation and thirst; some of them pleaded with the guards to shoot. When, at six in the morning, the time came for the cell to be opened, the guards could not open the door as it was blocked with dead bodies. Only 23 (including the woman) of the 146 were still living. Complained to by the survivors, the Nawab refused even to discuss what had happened.

The Black Hole atrocity greatly strengthened the British determination to recapture Calcutta and to obtain revenge on the Nawab. To cut short an extremely intricate story, Clive marched up from Madras and, without excessive difficulty, re-occupied Calcutta and signed a treaty with the Nawab, who was forced to pay compensation. Then, in diplomacy of tortuous complexity, Clive went on to plot the Nawab's replacement by his uncle, Mir Jaffir. Clive's personal reward was to be £250,000, which Mir Jaffir would pay him on achieving the throne. Lesser payments were arranged for other British officers and company officials and £300,000 was promised to an Indian intermediary, Omichand, who had once worked for the company but had been dismissed for peculation. In fact Clive perpetrated an out-right swindle on Omichand by preparing two copies of the treaty with Mir Jaffir, only one of which showed Omichand's bribe. One British officer, Admiral Watson, refused to be a party to such deceit and so Clive forged his signature. When eventually Omichand was told he would receive no money, he was so upset that he fell into a rapid decline and died, bequeathing what fortune he had to the London Foundling Hospital.

The battle of Plassey

With a force of 3,000 men, Clive marched against the Nawab's army, which was encamped by the village of Plassey, about a hundred miles north of Calcutta. Against Clive's 3,000, the Nawab, according to the customarily given figures, disposed of 40,000 infantry, 20,000 cavalry and 53 large guns manned by Frenchmen. Clive had hoped that a reinforcement of 10,000 men would be provided by Mir Jaffir but these failed to turn up. He hesitated to carry on without them and, in fact, his council of war voted by a majority in favour of withdrawal. After the council, Clive paced up and down on his own in a mango grove under the midday sun and then, to everybody's surprise, gave the order to keep on advancing towards Plassey. The next morning he changed his mind and ordered a halt. Then a message came – false as it turned out – that Mir Jaffir would fight with his 10,000 men after all. Clive resumed the advance.

The battle opened with a disastrous artillery exchange. The Nawab's guns were bigger and more numerous than those of Clive and pinned down the British. Then, by a stroke of luck, the monsoon broke and the Nawab's gunpowder became drenched and unusable. Clive had had the foresight to order the British powder to be kept under tarpaulin, and so his guns kept firing. The British charged and the Nawab's forces crumbled to pieces and fled from the field. The British lost twenty-three killed (seven British and sixteen Indian) while the Nawab lost over 500 dead and, more significantly, his whole army ceased to be an effective instrument. Shortly afterwards he was murdered by his uncle. Plassey, in 1757, marked the start of a British Empire in India which was to last 190 years until the last British regiments marched out to the tune 'Will ye no come back again?'

The treasure-chest of Bengal

Clive now had a British puppet on the throne of Bengal, the richest province in India. It was the size of France and its capital, Murshidabad, was bigger and infinitely more splendid than London. Within days of Mir Jaffir taking over, 200 chests filled with gold and jewels were sent down the river to Calcutta as the first installment of Clive's share in the loot. The word 'loot' was a Hindu one which passed into the English language in this period, and for good reason. Bengal lay wide open for plunder; the British bled her with a rapacity that can rarely have been excelled. Perhaps the nearest parallel was that of the Spanish in Mexico two centuries earlier. Clive himself made the biggest fortune of all but everyone else in the British service followed his example.

Besides straightforward robbery, the British conducted forced trade deals with unnaturally high profits and virtually took over the elaborate internal customs service by which they mulched ordinary Indians of dues at check-points on the highways. Later, after Clive had returned home, they deposed Mir Jaffir and, in exchange for bribes, installed another ruler in his place. Then, in exchange for yet further payments, they put Mir Jaffir back again. Clive himself obtained the neatest perquisite of all. As a reward for winning Plassey, Mir Jaffir gave him part of the land on which Calcutta stood and which was rented at £30,000 a year by the East India Company; this was a possession Clive could count safe against all the vagaries of Indian politics.

Many years later, Clive claimed that he had not been so

Above: *Surajah Dowlah,
Nawab of Bengal who, claiming
that the fortifications of the city
were aimed against him and that
the British were planning to
overthrow him, decided to take
over the British settlement of
Calcutta. He was responsible for
one of the most notorious
atrocities in British history, the
Black Hole of Calcutta* (left), *and
less directly, for the strengthening
of British power, as Clive was not
long in taking his revenge.*

These two Indian paintings show
the pleasant life to which British
officers in India were accustomed
when not actually in combat.
Above: *an officer with his
troops*; left: *Mahodaji Sindhia
entertains officers in his Delhi
home.*

rapacious as he could have been and had taken only what was legitimately due for services rendered. Defending himself against a critical committee of inquiry set up by the House of Commons, Clive said: 'Consider the situation in which the victory of Plassey had placed me. A great prince was dependent on my pleasure; an opulent city lay at my mercy; its richest bankers bid against each other for my smiles; I walked through vaults which were thrown open to me alone, piled on either hand with gold and jewels. By God, Mr Chairman, at this moment I stand astonished at my own moderation.'

Moderation or not, the sudden accession of almost the whole wealth of Bengal to British hands seems to have exerted a powerful influence upon the British domestic economy. Nabobs had been coming home rich from India for over half a century; now the supply increased and they were even richer. This was just at the time when mechanical inventions were making possible mass-production industry, especially in textiles. The wealth from India provided much of the capital for the eighteenth century industrial revolution which made Britain the richest country in the world. Without the Indian connection there might never have been a British industrial revolution or it might have come more slowly. Of course it was largely on the basis of the new industrial economy that the further colossal expansion of the British Empire took place in the reign of Queen Victoria.

Clive himself came home with such wealth that he was reckoned to be the richest British subject. He bought six palatial mansions in various parts of England and travelled through Europe to acquire paintings, tapestries, carpets and dinner services to put in them. He outbid the king of Poland for paintings by Paolo Veronese, Salvator Rosa and Claude Vernet. The only thing he would not buy, although he could easily have done so by contributing to political funds, was a title. He maintained that he should have a title for nothing, as a recognition of his services to the British Empire. From the very beginning, however, the British had their doubts about Clive, and all he received was the lowest possible kind of peerage, an Irish baronetcy, which carried no seat in the House of Lords. Clive bought a village in Ireland and changed its name to Plassey so he could be 'Lord Clive of Plassey' and bought seven seats in the House of Commons, one for himself and the others to form the nucleus of a Clive political party. He hoped for high ministerial office. He even attempted a take-over for the East India Company itself, but this failed.

Although he had fame and money, Clive had very little power in terms of British politics. He was flashy and dogmatic, unwilling and unable to adapt himself to London ways. Meanwhile under his successor Henry Vansittart Bengal was falling into chaos and stories of the greed of the British officials there were percolating home and causing a national scandal. Clive decided to give up his London ambitions, return to Bengal and re-establish order. He virtually drew up his own commission from the East India Company as governor and went out with near-absolute powers.

The new rulers

Back in Calcutta, Clive decided it was time to drop the pretence of a puppet Nawab of Bengal and for the company to take over the administration directly. He signed a treaty with the Moghul emperor by which the latter, in return for a subsidy of £500,000 a year, appointed the company 'Diwan of Bengal'. The last Nawab, a teenage boy who thought of nothing but women, was pensioned off and died almost immediately. The main right of the 'Diwan' was to collect taxes, and this Clive's men did with an efficiency never before known. The proceeds were divided between the company, the emperor and the local administration of Bengal, which remained largely in Indian hands; doubt-

less some of the proceeds also stuck to the hands of the British 'collectors'. The title 'collector'—although not the dubious methods associated with its origin—remained until the end of British rule the ordinary title of a British district officer in Bengal. In fact it is still in use under the modern Republic of India.

As a sort of poacher turned gamekeeper, Clive made some effort to check the peculation and illegitimate private trading that was going on. This, naturally, caused resentment, the officials considering that Lord Clive had no right to prevent others building up a fortune like his own. However Clive forced a 'trading syndicate', a kind of co-operative undertaking by which the officials pooled their private trade under some measure of supervision from Clive. Evidence of the huge profits that Clive himself continued to make in this period is provided by the presents he sent home to his wife. They included a diamond ring costing 11,000 rupees, a box of diamonds, rubies and pearls costing 42,000 rupees, a ruby ring set with diamonds, 103 loose pearls, 22 loose diamond drops and 11 bundles of fine muslins. He claimed, however, that this last spell in India left him £5,816 out of pocket after he had met all his expenses.

In 1767, at the age of forty-two, Clive left India for the last time. He was broken in health, suffering agonies from a bowel complaint, and was subject to fits of melancholia. Back in England the House of Commons appointed a committee to inquire into his career and damaging charges were made against him. At one moment it looked as if Clive were going to have to forfeit £234,000 which, it was calculated, he had acquired illegitimately. He died suddenly when he was only forty-nine, and rumour had it that his valet had found him with his throat cut. The alternative possibility is that he died of an overdose of opium, taken carelessly or on purpose. His grave was unmarked, and for the first century after his death the only memorial to him was at Shrewsbury. Even his name disappeared, his son taking the surname of Herbert to fit that of the earldom of Powis, whose heiress he married.

Clive's career cannot be understood solely in terms of his military genius or solely in terms of his love of money and power. The underlying factor was the particular state of India at that particular moment. The odds at Plassey as at many other battles, were such that Clive and other European commanders could only have won through the defects of their opponents. The Moslem dynasties of India, themselves originally alien invaders, were in an advanced state of decay. That Clive paid the Moghul emperor for the Bengal diwanate did not mean that the emperor had any effective power over Bengal, but merely that Clive wanted some show of legal sanction to cover what he was doing. Had things gone slightly differently, the French would have conquered India. Indeed the original aim of Napoleon Bonaparte was to do so, and to set himself up as its independent emperor. As it was, the opportunity fell to the British who, it must be remembered, conquered India with largely Indian troops. Time after time Indian soldiers under British command and training defeated much larger numbers of Indians under Indian leadership.

The original Clive establishment in Bengal turned out to be ridiculous. While its employees were making fortunes, the East India Company itself was losing money through its administration of Bengal and had to apply to the British government for a £400,000 a year subsidy to balance its books. Bengal itself, hitherto so rich and plentiful a province that it was known as the 'Garden of Eden', was devastated by a disastrous series of famines in which millions died. While obviously British depredations were not the cause of the rains failing, the actions of some British traders in hoarding and speculating in rice did not help the situation, and it could be held that the general debilitaion of the Bengal economy weakened its capacity to withstand food shortage. In the first direct British government intervention into Indian affairs, legislation was passed in 1774 to set up a governor-general, at the head of all British India, together with a council and law courts.

Warren Hastings

The first governor-general, Warren Hastings, was seven years Clive's junior and, like Clive, had started as a junior clerk with the East India Company. Unlike Clive, he was well-educated, and he took much trouble to master Indian languages and Indian culture. Clive spoke no Indian language at all, beyond a few essential words of command, but Hastings knew Urdu, Hindi and Persian, the latter being the court language at Delhi. While Clive, obviously, was a freebooter on the make, Hastings was a much more ambiguous character. Indeed his eleven years as governor-general formed a sort of bridge between the nabob methods of the eighteenth century and the uncorrupt Indian Civil Service of the eighteenth.

Hastings made some fortune in India – he had amassed £40,000 by the age of thirty – but he repressed the worst forms of graft and made some start in building up a settled administration. He faced many difficulties. He was saddled with a curious constitution by which he could be outvoted in his own council – he fought a duel with one member of it – and the presidencies of Madras and Bombay, although nominally subordinate to his administration at Calcutta, conducted semi-independent policies and could appeal direct to London over his head. It was because of initiative from Bombay that he was forced into a war which extended the company's territories in central India. To pay for the war, he extracted levies from Indian rulers; if they refused to pay up, he invaded their territories and took what he wanted. He repelled a fresh French attempt to obtain power in India.

In the most controversial action of all he hanged for forgery a Bengali merchant called Nandu Kumar who had accused *him* of forgery. This was an action of the most doubtful legality since forgery was not a capital offence in Indian law, although it was in British law. The chief justice at Calcutta, Elijah Impey, had been Hastings's fag at Westminster School.

Back in England there were parliamentary criticisms of Hastings's actions and in 1784 the prime minister, William Pitt the Younger, introduced legislation to bring the Calcutta administration under yet closer British government control. Hastings resigned in protest and arrived back in London in 1785 to find himself accused of corruption and extortion. He was impeached in 1787. Impeachment was an obsolescent procedure by which the House of Commons prosecuted a major political personality before the House of Lords, who acted as judges. It had been a significant weapon in constitutional struggles in the past, but had not been employed for a century and has never subsequently been employed. In theory Hastings was liable to suffer any punishment from death downwards. Because of the volume and complexity of the evidence and because the hearings were adjourned whenever parliament adjourned, the trial lasted seven years. In the end Hastings was acquitted. He had spent, he claimed, the bulk of his fortune on defending himself, but he lived on for thirty years more in peaceful retirement on money that had inherited from his family.

Under the new Pitt legislation, the governor-general of India was appointed by the British government, and was responsible primarily to that government. He should be a British aristocrat with a mind above making a personal profit out of his office. The first governor-general under the new regime was Lord Cornwallis the same man who had surrendered to the Americans at Yorktown – and many expected him to be a failure. In fact, however, he worked well and established the foundations of the Victorian method of governing India. Britain was already the strongest power in the sub-continent, and in a series of wars and annexations under Cornwallis and his successors she automatically extended her dominion until no authority independent of her existed.

Clive's meeting with Mir Jaffir, uncle of the Nawab of Bengal, after the Battle of Plassey, at which the Nawab's forces were completely defeated. Plassey, in 1757, marked the start of the British Empire in India – Clive now had a puppet on the throne of Bengal, the richest province in the country.

Right: *Shah Alam handing to Robert Clive the formal grant of sovereign rights in Bengal, in 1765. This grant virtually made the East India Company rulers of Bengal, though Clive himself had doubts about the ability of the company to undertake such responsibility, and had already suggested that the British Crown should assume sovereignty.*

Robert Clive's youth, distinguished by unpleasant and dishonest behaviour, gave little indication of the astonishing success he was later to achieve. After a disastrous year as a clerk with the East India Company he entered the military service, and it was as a military commander that he discovered his true genius. His capture of Arcot, and the part he played in the seige of Trichinopoly thwarted Dupleix and marked the end of French power in India.

71

The trial of Hastings, who resigned in 1785 in protest against
measures to bring the Calcutta administration under closer British
control, and returned home to find himself charged with corruption and
extortion. He was impeached two years later, and the trial dragged on
for seven years before his eventual acquittal. Right: a satire of the
impending impeachment of Hastings. Hastings is seated on the camel in
oriental dress, while Burke fires a blunderbuss at the shield of honour.
Behind are Fox and North.

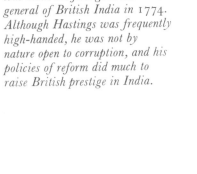

Warren Hastings, who became Governor of Bengal in 1772, and was made the first governor-general of British India in 1774. Although Hastings was frequently high-handed, he was not by nature open to corruption, and his policies of reform did much to raise British prestige in India.

Below: *the storming of Seringapatam, 1799. It was left to Wellesley, who became governor-general in 1798, to put paid to Tipu Sultan, who now, backed by Napoleon, and busily assembling a French-trained army, presented an even greater threat to Britain. Wellesley offered him a treaty under which he would dismiss the Frenchmen and disband his troops, but Tipu chose to fight. He was killed in 1799 at his capital Seringapatam.*

The Nelson touch

Horatio Nelson, who won the most decisive sea battles in British history, epitomizes Britain's sea power in the eighteenth century. At this time the Royal Navy, staffed by highly skilled and experienced officers, was the most effective fighting force in the world, rightly feared by other nations.

The first great burst of European exploration of the rest of the world occurred in the fifteenth and sixteenth centuries. It was in this period that America and the Pacific were discovered, the coastline of Africa was charted and the sea routes were opened to India, China and Japan. There still, however, remained enormous gaps in the Europeans' knowledge of world geography.

During a lull of over a century, relatively little further exploration, on a major scale, took place. Geographers attempted to fill in the gaps in exact knowledge with ingenious theorising. For example they held that there 'must' be a great continent in the southern hemisphere to 'balance' the known land masses in the northern hemisphere. They held that gold 'must' be at its most plentiful around the Equator. This theory about gold was of some practical significance because it acted as a disincentive to further ocean exploration: what could be the point of sailing off into unknown dangers when science taught that there was little chance of finding gold at the end of them?

Eighteenth century exploration

The revival of ocean exploration in the eighteenth century completed the outline map of most of the world's coastlines. By 1800, there were human beings who for the first time in history, had a roughly correct idea of what their whole planet looked like. This was the most important milestone towards mankind's knowledge of his environment until space travel started in the mid-twentieth century. In the first explorations of the fifteenth and sixteenth centuries the Spanish, the Portuguese, the Dutch and, as individuals, the Italians, had been in the lead. The British in that period had been as much pirates, preying on others' discoveries, as explorers. Now, in the new phase, the British were clearly the leaders in world exploration.

In 1730 the Englishman John Hadley invented the sextant, which for the first time enabled a ship to plot its position in the open ocean with some exactitude, and it was mainly British medical experimentation which established lime juice as a preventative for scurvy, the vitamin-deficiency disease which on long voyages made sailors' teeth drop out, and sometimes even killed them.

The initiative came primarily from the aggressive British Admiralty which, for motives both scientific and strategic, wanted to be able to use at will all the oceans of the world. The aim was not, perticularly, to establish colonies, save as supply bases for a world-wide Royal Navy, but rather to build up strength against other European powers. The third British Empire grew up alongside the American and Indian ones as an accidental by-product of this process.

The process began with voyages that were of interest rather than importance. William Dampier, on an Admiralty commission, sailed three times around the world at the turn of the seventeenth and eighteenth centuries: he and his men were the first Englishmen to sight the coast of Australia, though the Dutch and, possibly, the Portuguese had seen it already. Thirty years after Dampier's activities, Admiral George Anson sailed around the world with a squadron of six warships; his motive was not exploration but to plunder the Spanish colonies during the War of the Austrian Succession. Anson seized treasure worth £500,000, but he lost five-sixths of his men, mainly through disease and hardship, and only one of his ships, commanded by James Cook, eventually got back to England. It was this man who was to make a series of three decisive voyages.

Captain Cook

The first man of humble social origin to play a major role in the creation of the British Empire, Cook was undoubtedly a genius. Seaman, scientist and leader of men, he was born at the bottom of the social scale as the son of a farm labourer, and started his

Captain Cook rapidly overcame the disadvantage of his humble origins to play a major role in the creation of the British Empire. A natural leader of men, and by far the best navigator and cartographer of his day, he was nevertheless quiet and reserved, his only close friend being the scientist Joseph Banks, who sailed with him.

The dispersal of hostile tribes near Baines River. The Aborigines of Australia were regarded by the settlers as less than human, and were rapidly cleared off the land—occasionally they were even hunted for sport. Unlike the American Indians, they made no attempt to fight back.

working life as a grocer's apprentice. He then went to sea, starting as an ordinary seaman, in a coaster which carried coal from Newcastle to London. By his early twenties he was a mate.

Cook turned down an opportunity to command a coaster to enlist in the Royal Navy as an ordinary seaman. He rapidly rose to be a master's mate and then a master; these were ranks connected with the navigation and technical handling of a warship and were subordinate to the commissioned captain and his lieutenants who commanded it. Most able men of Cook's class never reached commissioned rank, and even as brilliant an officer as Cook was scaling enormous social barriers in doing so; not until he was forty-seven, and had completed two epoch-making voyages of discovery, did he reach the rank of captain.

Although he was famous in his own day and many first-hand accounts of him are available, it is difficult to evaluate his true character and motivations. All accounts of him are adulatory and reveal little of him as a human being; if they are to be taken as comprehensive, he never did anything discreditable. He was a reserved man who spent most of his adult life at sea; his marriage took place after only six weeks courtship and he was away during most of it. As a young officer he devoted himself, quietly, to the intensive study of mathematics and navigation – he was by far the best navigator and chart-maker of his day – and, as an older man in command of a ship, he preserved the dignity and distance proper for maintaining a captain's authority on a long voyage. His only close friend was the scientist Joseph Banks, who sailed with him. Banks made it clear to everyone that he regarded James Cook as the greatest man he had ever met.

The discomforts and dangers of an eighteenth-century voyage of exploration were far worse than have so far been encountered in the exploration of space. Crews were crammed into small ships for years on end. They needed the skills of acrobats to change sails in a storm. Food was salt beef and biscuit – it was customary to tap one's biscuit before eating it so that the weevils would crawl out – and the only treat was a daily tot of rum. Scurvy was a continuous menace. A captain risked losing his whole crew through disease – as Anson lost most of his – or through mutiny, as Cook's contempory William Bligh did on the *Bounty*.

Part of Cook's genius lay in his methods of management. He was not unduly gentle and, like all other British captains of the time, made use of the savage cat-of-nine-tails when he considered it necessary. But he systematically cared for his men's health. He had fires lit on the foetid messdecks to make draughts of fresh air to purify them. He burned gunpowder as a disinfectant. He took a stock of German pickled cabbage which he made the men eat every day to keep up their health. Such measures were the necessary basis of his success.

Cook first attracted attention when he took part in Wolfe's expedition against Quebec. He was one of the group of navigators who performed the daring feat of taking 200 ships up the dangerous St Lawrence river without loss. He stayed on in North America to make a series of charts of the waters around Newfoundland. These confirmed his scientific reputation at the Admiralty in London and in 1768 he was commissioned as a lieutenant and given command of the *Endeavour*, a little ship that was to sail to the Pacific and observe the transit of Venus between earth and sun, due in 1769.

This first great voyage of Cook's lasted three years. The astronomical side of it was a comparative failure; what mattered was that the discoveries he made during the voyage established the correct geography of about a quarter of the world's surface. What had been an area of theoretical speculation was converted into an area of scientific fact. Cook was not a total pioneer – the French Louis de Bougainville and the British Samuel Wallis had been his immediate predecessors in surveying the Pacific – but

his work eclipsed everyone else's. He discovered, charted and named whole strings of Pacific islands, thus bringing their isolated inhabitants into contact with the rest of the world. Cook quite definitely regarded them as 'savages' but he was humane and courteous towards them. He established the shape of New Zealand by sailing right around it and landing on it. He named New South Wales in Australia, and landed at Botany Bay there. He charted about half the Australian coast, being the first man to establish the size and shape of it. He annexed both Australia and New Zealand to the British crown.

Thus, while his contemporaries in India were looting Bengal and his contemporaries in America were moving towards the War of Independence, Cook was calmly adding gigantic new territories to the British Empire. The only personal profit he made was his naval pay, to which small bonuses were added, and the royalties from the sale of the books he wrote.

He spent less than a year at home in England before setting out on a second three-year voyage in which he charted most of the southern Pacific, penetrating below the Antarctic circle, and discovered more islands. Again, after less than a year at home, Cook started his third voyage which, potentially, was to be the longest and most important of all. The aim was the old one of trying to find a north-west sea passage across the north of the north American continent. He sailed up the western coast of Canada, around Alaska, through the Bering Strait (which had been discovered by a Swede, Vitus Bering, serving in the Russian navy), and into the Arctic where the ice prevented him getting any further northwards. Cook turned away from the ice and went southwards by way of the Siberian coast, as always charting it, and then made for Hawaii in the mid-Pacific, an apparently congenial place which provided women for his crew. On February 14, 1799, through an accidental quarrel arising from a misunderstanding, a group of Hawaians attacked him on the beach at Kealekua Bay and hacked him to pieces. All that could be recovered of him – his skull, his hands and a few bones – were buried at sea. It took nine months for the news of his death to reach London.

Founding of Australia

The British were vaguely pleased to have acquired a sub-continent on the opposite side of the world, but were none too clear what to do with it. At first it was just a useful place for sending criminals to – after the War of Independence it was no longer possible to send them in servitude to the American colonies. Now they could be sent instead to New South Wales. Thus in 1787, eighteen years after Cook anchored in Botany Bay, a fleet of ten ships set out from England to establish what has now grown into the nation of Australia. The first Australians were 717 convicts and 200 marine guards. The new settlement had a governor of high ability, Captain Arthur Phillip from the Royal Navy. He was a tense, thin little man who had a vision of founding a permanent new community, not just running a convict prison. The original idea had been to settle at Cook's Botany Bay but, in fact, Phillip entered a harbour he recognised as 'the finest in the world'. He called it Sydney after the British secretary of state, Lord Sydney, who had sponsored the expedition, and there formed his settlement.

The population lived first in tents, then in huts and, ultimately, in proper houses. Phillip agitated for free immigrants, and several dozens came out, the convicts being assigned to them as labourers. Some of the convicts were hopelessly bad colonising material; they were products of the English slums, lacking in education and dumbly resentful of all society. Others, however, really wanted a new life, and within five years the first of them were released and given thirty acres of land each.

The native inhabitants of Australia, contemptuously referred

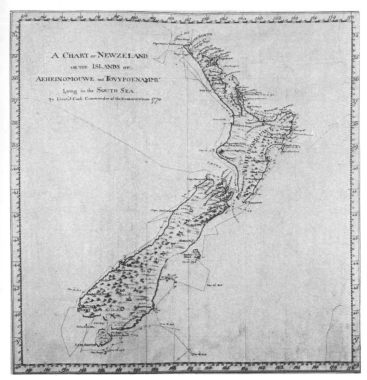

Cook's chart of New Zealand; The discoveries made by Cook on his voyages established the correct geography of about a quarter of the world. Having ascertained the shape of New Zealand by sailing round it, and charting about half the Australian coast, he annexed both countries for the British crown.

Captain Arthur Phillip, the first governor of New South Wales, a man of considerable vision who believed that his task was not just to rule a settlement of convicts, but 'to lay the foundations of a new Empire'.

The death of Captain Cook. On 14 February 1799 Cook was hacked to pieces by a group of Hawaians at Kealekua Bay as the result of a quarrel arising from a misunderstanding. Four marines were killed and three wounded before the remainder managed to escape.

A detail from a painting of a scene on Nelson's flagship, the HMS Victory, showing Nelson falling to the deck, mortally wounded, at the Battle of Trafalgar.

The Battle of the Nile. The complete destruction of the French fleet by Nelson at Aboukir Bay defeated Napoleon's plan to crush the British Empire by striking at Egypt, and ultimately, India.

to as the 'Aboriginals' were sparse in numbers and at a low technical stage of development. They were regarded as scarcely human and, in the settlement of Australia, were cleared off the land even more ruthlessly than the American Indians had been. They put up scarcely any resistance. On occasion the settlers actually hunted the 'Abos' for sport.

New Zealand was not, at this stage, settled at all. It had a relatively sophisticated native population, the Maoris, who certainly did not regard themselves as having been annexed by the British. The first real contacts did not come until 1815, when British missionaries entered New Zealand with a view to converting the inhabitants to Protestant Christianity.

Cook's heir, so far as he had one, was George Vancouver, who had served as a lieutenant under him on his second and third voyages. Vancouver, an East Anglican of remote Dutch descent, was a stern disciplinarian and none too popular. In the 1790s he further surveyed the Pacific and, in 1792, charted what is now the western coast of Canada. The latter was to be of some importance for the future as it staked out this area for British-Canadian settlement rather than Russian (the Russians were already established in Alaska and remained there until 1867 when they sold the territory to the United States).

The British Navy

By the end of the eighteenth century, the British Royal Navy had reached a level of skill and experience which made it the most effective sea fighting force in the world. The officers, drawn mostly from the minor gentry, had high technical qualifications. They started learning their profession as children, going to sea when they were eleven or twelve. Their pay was only moderate but they always had the hope of winning a fortune in prize money. In the army, commissions were bought and sold, but in the navy the criterion for promotion up to the rank of captain was mainly merit, tempered a little by the fact that an officer with family or friendly connections with politicians or the Admiralty had a distinct advantage.

A captain was the complete autocrat of his ship, with powers of life and death if he was on detached service. Some naval captains were cruel or eccentric, but the majority were sound professionals, without whom there could never have been a British Empire. Promotion above the rank of captain was entirely by seniority, a quaint system which meant that admirals were sometimes aged men who had not been to sea for years. When an admiral died or was 'yellowed' (equivalent to retired), the senior captain on the list stepped up to rear-admiral. Only the fact that Admiralty influence got him promoted to captain at the exceptionally early age of twenty-two enabled Horatio Nelson to reach admiral's rank in time to win the most significant sea battles in British history.

Under the commissioned officers in the navy existed a tough capable class of long-service warrant officers and petty officers. They included the masters and master's mates (responsible for navigating a ship), the gunners, the boatswains and their mates (responsible for discipline), the carpenters, the sailmakers, the clerks and the quartermasters. Commissioned officers were posted from ship to ship but the senior warrant officers often remained in the same ship for their whole working lives, perhaps twenty or thirty years.

Unlike modern military equipment, the warships of the eighteenth and early nineteenth centuries were slow to become

Left: 'The first Parliament of Botany Bay in High Debate.' The discovery of this huge tract of almost uninhabited land solved the British government's problem of what to do with its criminals, who could no longer be sent in servitude to the American colonies. In 1787 the first fleet of convict ships was sent out from England to establish a settlement at Botany Bay, and within five years, under the able leadership of Captain Arthur Phillip, many of the convicts had been released and given their own land to work.

Below: *Arthur Wellesley, 1st Duke of Wellington, whose great victory over Napoleon at Waterloo finally extinguished the threat from France.*

obsolescent. Nelson's flagship at Trafalgar, H.M.S. *Victory*, was in active commission for almost a century. The wooden, sail-powered ship-of-the-line, with its tiers of cannon and soaring masts, had reached such a point of technical perfection that most naval officers regarded steam-powered ships, of which the first was built in 1802, as mere curiosities.

The problem with the sailing warships—by the time of the Napoleonic wars in the early nineteenth century Britain had over 300 of them in commission—was that they needed huge crews of up to 1,000 seamen so that simultaneously all guns could be manned while sails were being changed, with a margin of spare men available to fill gaps caused by battle casualties and disease. The ships were not really big enough to carry such numbers and, as a result, the ordinary seamen lived, sometimes

for years on end, in extreme discomfort. They slept in tiers of hammocks with often only eighteen inches of space for each man. Naturally it was difficult to get volunteers for such arduous service. Some joined because they could get no other work. Some had a sense of ambition, patriotism and adventure, plus a hope of prize money. Many, especially when the navy inflated its size in wartime, were conscripted by the press gang.

Theoretically only professional seamen were liable to be seized by the Royal Navy, but in practice, at times of manpower shortage, almost any man of the lower social classes was liable to be seized in the street and forced on board ship in conditions near to slavery. Once aboard he could be kept there for years on end; even when a ship touched port, the crew might not be allowed ashore for fear of desertion. A man who deserted and was recaptured was hanged, if he was lucky, or else was 'flogged around the fleet', a punishment which could be equivalent to death by torture. The Emperor Napoeon I of the French could never understand the British penchant for flogging their sailors and soldiers; he considered it the opposite of sound management. There were a couple of naval mutinies which caused momentary frights to the British, but on the whole the system worked.

The threat from Napoleon

While Australia and New Zealand had been acquired by sheer exploring zeal and without conflict with any European power, the next round of British imperial acquisitions resulted from the exercise of sea power in yet another war between Britain and France.

The French Revolution, which started in 1789, was based on ideals of liberty, political equality and modernisation. It culminated in the execution of King Louis XVI, the mass execution of aristocrats and the establishment of a republic. Most of the upper classes throughout Europe, including those in Britain, were horrified at these events.

Although the British had a parliamentary system of government, they were certainly not a democracy; only a minority of the population had the right to vote, and real power rested in an alliance of landowners with city of London businessmen, plus some of the Indian nabobs who had bought their way in from the plunder of Bengal. The hereditary monarchy and the hereditary House of Lords were both real political forces. Thus although some British radicals sympathised with the French revolution, British power was, effectively, ranged against it.

From 1793 to 1815 Europe was almost continuously at war, the British and the French being on opposite sides. The causes of the war were, partly, the sheer vigour of the French in their desire to 'liberate' Europe and to build up the glory of their state and, partly, a desire by the conservative powers to put down the revolution and restore the French monarchy. On the land, the French won most of the time but the British, who as a result of their early industrial revolution were the world's richest power, kept subsidising new alliances.

Liberty is often an early casualty of war, and with the coming to power of the emperor Napoleon I the French Revolution lost its more democratic aspects. However, it continued to be a vital modernising force in Europe, sweeping away the remnants of feudalism and reforming methods of law and administration. Napoleon, born in Corsica, was more of an Italian than a Frenchman. He was a soldier and administrator of genius who in his youth had once thought of joining the British army in India. He went into the French army which, after the revolution, gave him the opportunity to rise rapidly. After major victories in Italy, he set off with an army to conquer Egypt. He had some idea of going on to conquer India and setting himself up there as an independent ruler. However, Nelson destroyed his fleet in the Battle of the Nile and he returned to France where he seized power as First Consul. Four years later after a plebiscite he took the royal title of Emperor of the French.

At the height of his power, Napoleon directly controlled France, Italy, Poland and the Rhineland, and had members of his family on the thrones of Holland and Spain. The emperors of Russia and Austria and the king of Prussia were his allies. Only the British opposed him. Then, seeing signs of truculence from the Emperor of Russia, Napoleon invaded Russia, but failed to establish effective control. His army was destroyed by the Russian winter and his system fell to pieces. Egged on by the British, Austria and Prussia joined forces against him and in 1814 he abdicated. A year later he returned to France but was defeated by combined British and Prussian armies at Waterloo. He was exiled to the mid-Atlantic island of St Helena.

Napoleon had had a dream of 'liberating' the British by armed invasion, and in 1804 had assembled an army at Boulogne for this purpose. Had he been able to cross the English Channel he would certainly have won a military victory, there being only a handful of troops in Britain. He could possibly even have established some kind of government in London, although it is difficult to imagine the British radicals accepting one of the Bonaparte brothers as their king. However, the strength of the British navy made him change his mind, and instead he turned east to win his great victory over Austria at Austerlitz.

New acquisitions and further expansion

Britain's invulnerability against invasion was consolidated in 1805 when Nelson destroyed the combined French and Spanish fleets off Cape Trafalgar, Spain. Thereafter the British were free to roam the oceans, picking up new bases and colonies as side-actions to the war in Europe. In the Mediterranean they acquired Malta – the inhabitants actually petitioned for British protection. In the West Indies they conquered Trinidad and in South America they acquired British Guiana (now Guyana). In Africa they took over Cape Colony from the Dutch, and in the Indian Ocean they conquered Mauritius from France; the two last were regarded as essential for guarding the route to India. They picked up Java and the great island of Ceylon from the Dutch – Holland throughout the wars was an integral part of Napoleon's system.

At the end of the wars, the British kept all their new possessions with the exception of Java, which they gave back to the Dutch. There was very little discussion about it and certainly no thought that the populations should be consulted on whether they wanted to join the British Empire. But, then, in settling the frontiers of Europe, the wishes of the populations were, at the most, only of secondary importance. As an afterthought, after the wars were over, the British gobbled up the extra morsel of the mid-Atlantic island of Tristan da Cunha, lest it be used as a base from which to attempt a rescue of Napoleon.

In India, too, the wars caused further British expansion. The fear that Napoleon might break through from Egypt was an incentive to the British to consolidate and extend their power and to eliminate the vestiges of French influence. The motives were primarily political and not directly commercial. Governor-General Lord Wellesley, aided by his younger brother, the future Duke of Wellington, forced treaties on to Indian princes which made them clients of the British, and conquered Tipu, the powerful Sultan of Mysore, who had recruited French officers into his army.

By 1805 Britain had finally become the paramount power in the Indian sub-continent, although Wellesley was less than popular with the East India Company because his policy was financially unprofitable. Ceylon, geographically an appendage of India, was kept administratively distinct as a crown colony and not added to the East India Company territories. The Dutch had controlled only the coast but in 1815 the British pushed inland and absorbed the ancient Buddhist kingdom of Kandy, which represented a culture stretching back continuously to the fifth century BC.

Thus despite the loss of the United States of America, by the beginning of the nineteenth century Britain had become the world's leading colonising power. In terms of actual territory, Spain, which had most of South America, was still the larger power but the Spanish empire was on the point of disintegrating, whereas the British Empire was only in the early stage of a colossal expansion. From 1815 to 1918, more and more territory was added to the British Empire, toeholds were converted into full-scale colonies, until the British commanded a quarter of the world.

View of the Cape of Good Hope, and the battle of 1806 by which Britain took the territory from the Dutch. Like Mauritius, Cape Colony was regarded as essential for guarding the route to India. Opposition to British rule later led to the Great Trek of 1835–36 in which Boer farmers migrated northwards to found Natal, Traansvaal and the Orange Free State.

Grand Harbour, Malta. After Nelson's victory at Trafalgar, which effectively destroyed the French and Spanish fleets, Britain had the freedom of the oceans, and was able to acquire new bases and colonies. The inhabitants of Malta petitioned for British protection after Napoleon had taken possession of the island in 1798. The French were forced to surrender after a two-year siege, and in 1813 the Maltese were acknowledged as British subjects.

Wider still and wider

Immigrants arrive in New Zealand, a lithograph by W. Alsworth. In the late eighteenth and throughout the nineteenth century huge numbers of Europeans made their way to the colonies to start new lives. The largest proportion of emigrants were from Britain and Ireland, where drastic social change together with population increase brought severe hardship to many.

Three enormous movements of population exploded out of Europe in the nineteenth century. One was the steady expansion of the Russian Empire from its European territories southwards into central Asia and eastwards towards Siberia and China. In the Soviet Union, the successor state to the Russian Empire, Russians are a minority of the total population. Throughout the nineteenth century a fear that Russia would come to dominate the Middle East by swallowing up Turkey, and would attempt to enter India through Afghanistan were dominating influences in British policy, and some British colonies, notably Cyprus, were acquired primarily to stop Russia from seizing them.

There was only one actual war between Britain and Russia, that in the Crimea in the middle of the nineteenth century, and in it the British and the French appeared in the historically surprising position of allies, but friction between the two powers was a continuing factor. The Russian expansion halted with the Russo-Japanese war of 1905 which, contrary to all expectation, the Japanese won. That an Asiatic power could defeat a European one was a novel idea and a portent for the future (of course the Soviet Union acquired further territory as a result of the Second World War and constructed a system of satellite states).

The second great European expansion was westwards, across the Atlantic, to form the modern United States of America. At the start of the nineteenth century the United States was reasonably prosperous for its size but it was only a weak group of former colonies clustered on the eastern edge of the North American continent. It was no real embarrassment for the British when, in 1812, the American's took Napoleon's side in the war because of British interference with their shipping. There were some small-scale naval encounters and the British burned down official buildings in the new capital, Washington. By the end of the nineteenth century the United States had spread across the continent.

The key to the start of this process was the Louisiana purchase, by which the United States bought Louisiana from Napoleon I for $15 million, Napoleon having decided that his destiny lay in Europe, not America. In this purchase the Americans obtained not only what is now the state of Louisiana but also, in effect, their whole western hinterland. Throughout the century, by right of what was called 'manifast destiny', the Americans spread westwards, sweeping aside the Indian inhabitants. The American Declaration of Independence describes the Indians as 'savages' and they were treated as such. Often the Indians fought back fiercely, but they were too few in numbers – under one million in all – to keep the sub-continent for themselves.

Population and emigration

The population to fulfill the 'manifest destiny' came from Europe, the largest proportion being provided by Britain and Ireland. It was an almost continuously increasing flood which reached its peak in the first decade of the twentieth century. One reason for this was that Britain had an extraordinarily high birth-rate: between 1750 and 1850, for no clear scientific reason, the population trebled from 7.7 million to 20.7 million. Other European populations also rose but on nothing like the same scale.

Together with its population growth, Britain passed through a savage social revolution, its yeomen being driven off the land by the process of 'enclosing' it to make large farms. Although this made for greater economic efficiency, it distorted the traditional social fabric in a manner which occurred nowhere else in Europe. In France the peasants' prosperity increased as a result of the revolution; in Britain social change eliminated them. The process was particularly thorough in the Scottish highlands, where the clan chiefs drove out their clan members to make way

Passengers on board an emigrant ship leaving Britain.

for sheep. In Ireland there was relatively little positive attempt to drive the peasants out, but a similar result was achieved by absentee British landlords, who took extortionate rents from the peasantry, and by misgovernment, which caused actual famines. Such was the national vigour of both British and Irish that, in millions, instead of sitting down and dying, they reacted to personal hardship by setting off to settle in the United States. Together with Italians, Germans, Poles, Greeks and many others (but relatively few French) they sought the opportunities of a new country. Most, in practice, remained in the east of America and it was only the most venturesome who went to shoot it out with the Indians and with each other in the far west.

The third wave of expansion, in addition to the Russian and American ones, was the acquiring of huge colonies far distant from their shores by western European countries. Here Britain, if only because of India, was by far the most active. The French came second, with their expansions into Indo-China and West Africa. The Germans and the Italians entered the scene later, largely for prestige reasons.

Unlike the Russian and American advances across a continuous land mass, the nineteenth-century British Empire was a scattered affair. Even the nearest colony to the motherland, Gibraltar, was over 1,000 miles away. It could take a year to send a message to India by sailing ship and receive an answer. While it would be premature to claim that either the Russian or American expansions have reached a point of stability, the British Empire, obviously, had far less than either.

Colonisation and settlement

The British Empire really took two distinct forms, and it is crucial to distinguish between them. There was an imperialism

which created wholly new countries, for example Australia, and there was an imperialism which involved the British assuming control of existing countries, of which the supreme example was India. Occasionally the two concepts became confused, as in southern Africa.

The original meaning of the word 'colony' was a group of nationals of the mother country emigrating to another land. Any question of ruling over an alien people was subsidiary to this purpose. Originally, as in America, British colonisation was entirely of this type. According to primitive imperialist economics, such a colony provided both market and raw materials for the home country. Also such a colony was a good way of disposing of the indigent or such dissident religious groups as the *Mayflower* party. The Spanish and the British were, really, the only European countries to set about systematic colonisation in this sense. The French had attempted it in the eighteenth century, as the existence of Quebec testifies, but thereafter, save in the special case of Algeria, they did not do so. The Germans made a half-hearted attempt in Africa. The British, however, were successful in Canada, Australia and New Zealand.

What was required for this kind of colonisation to succeed was a sparse, primitive indigenous race which would offer no substantial opposition. This was found in North America and in Australia. In New Zealand the Maoris were, for several decades, a definite obstacle, but eventually tolerant policies on both sides enabled British settlement to proceed. In the nineteenth century it was widely assumed that Africans, similarly, provided no obstacle to European settlement. It was assumed that they were, in real terms, harmless and that they would either die out or be

content with subsidiary status. As late as the 1950s, Sir Roy Welensky, Prime Minister of the Central African Federation, was warning Africans that they should not risk following the fate of the American Indians. The same kind of thought existed also in America, where imported Africans formed, as slaves, the basis of part of the infant American economy. In the 1870s a Mississippi preacher, Dr C. K. Marshall, commanded much attention with a prediction that the American Negroes would be extinct by 1920. In fact, however, Africans on both sides of the Atlantic were to display a wholly unexpected racial vitality. Out of all the attempts to form white colonies in Africa the only two remaining by the 1970s were South Africa and Rhodesia. The West Indies were a special case in that both whites and blacks were immigrants (the blacks originally as slaves) and the native inhabitants, the Caribs, were completely absorbed or wiped out.

A wholly different type of colonialism was that in which the British took over the administration of a people held to be incapable of ruling themselves, but did so with no idea of starting a new British community. In India and in most of the African colonies, the British came out in quite large numbers as officials, technicians, missionaries and businessmen together with their families but they always regarded themselves as expatriates. Even when a family served several generations in India, it continued to regard itself as British—this applied even up to the twentieth century, even when such a family had acquired Indian blood through intermarriage.

That there was no intention of setting up a permanent British community did not imply that the colonisation was intended to be temporary. During the hey-day of colonial acquisition in the

Above: *Sir John A. Macdonald, the first premier of the dominion of Canada. The federal union of Canada – the first in the British Empire – came into being on 1 July, 1867. Although the union of British provinces seemed the only way to ensure successful growth for the country as a whole, only four provinces entered the union at first (Ontario, Quebec, Nova Scotia and New Brunswick); Newfoundland, the last to join, did not do so until 1949.*

Left: *baptism of the Maori chief Te Puni in Otaki church, a painting by Charles Decimus Barraud. The first English missionaries, who landed in New Zealand in the early years of the nineteenth century, were hindered by murderous tribal wars and made slow progress in spreading Christianity. However, their patience and perseverance was eventually rewarded; by 1839 the island was mainly peaceful and Christianity was in the ascendant.*

nineteenth century it came to be held that the British had a special mission to rule 'inferior' peoples for their own good. The driving motives were partly strategic – that is to gain bases – partly a greed for trade and raw materials, partly a desire to win conversions to Protestant Christianity and partly ambition.

Canada

The model for the first type of colonisation, that of permanent settlement, was Canada which, in physical area, is the second largest country on earth. The 'original' Canadians were the French in Quebec. Then, after the American War of Independence – which was much more of a civil war than traditional American historians have been prepared to allow – some 70,000 'loyalists' from the American colonies migrated northwards to

Canada because they would not accept the rule of the Washington-Jefferson group.

Although the early nineteenth-century Canadians, both British and French, tended to be conservative in outlook, they disliked being ruled autocratically from London. The British element, in particular, wanted parliamentary institutions. After a rebellion in the 1830s, the London government sent out the radical Earl of Durham to examine the situation and in a report which must count as one of the major documents of the nineteenth century, he recommended the union of French and British Canada with an elected parliament. His immediate aim was to submerge raw French nationalism under British liberalism. But, in fact, radicals of both groups won the first election and the governor, Sir Charles Bagot, appointed their leaders to government office. Thus was inaugurated the system of 'responsible' government, that is a colonial administration being answerable directly to the elected legislature and dependent upon it for continuing in office.

Had such a device been conceived a century earlier it is possible that the American colonies would never have needed to renounce the British connection. Perhaps, by the twentieth century, the British monarch would have been residing in Washington and speaking with an American accent. The point was that in the eighteenth century nobody really realised how the British constitution was developing. In drafting their cumbersome American constitution, the American radicals thought they were constructing a purified version of the British system. They considered the notion of ministers being members of the legislature as a corruption and rigorously separated the executive from the legislative power. Actually the British system was developing towards all power being in the hands of a committee of the majority party in the elected House of Commons, with the nominal executive, the monarch, becoming powerless. The reality of this developed long before most observers recognised it; despite Bagehot's injunction that her function was only to be informed, to advise and to warn, Queen Victoria, to the end of her life, believed that she had a real share in running the country.

As local politicians in Canada obtained executive power, the connection between Canada and Britain became in real terms a solely voluntary arrangement. In the early nineteenth century the connection was still useful for Canada for purely military reasons of defence against the powerful and zestful United States to the south. The French-Canadians, in particular, feared that an American conquest of Canada would lead to the submerging of their linguistic and cultural identity. The possibility of American conquest was for long a reality and the United States declared war upon Britain in 1812 with the annexation of Canada as one of its aims. The Americans lost that war and a British expedition burned public buildings in the new American capital, Washington. (The president's official residence had to be painted white to conceal the marks of the fire that had gutted it and so it came to be known as the White House.)

For a further half century there was sporadic talk in the United States of 'liberating Canada' and of 'driving the English out of the Americas'. As late as 1870 Charles Sumner, chairman of the senate foreign relations committee, was demanding that the British should cede Canada to the United States in compensation for having accorded belligerent status to the south in the American civil war. However, the 3,500 mile frontier between the United States and Canada, most of it a straight line drawn on the map along the 49th degree of latitude, had been defined in 1846 and the Treaty of Washington of 1871 marked the end of American ambitions to expand northwards – they had plenty to absorb them in their gigantic western territories. There were a few local border disputes, caused by over-

First Train in Vancouver

The arrival of the first trans-Canada passenger train in Vancouver on the newly built Canadian Pacific railway, 1887. The sheer size of Canada was a serious drawback to political unity; before the railways were built, communications were almost non-existent, and vast areas of rich agricultural land were unexploited.

Hauling timber in the upper
Ottawa river region; Canada's
vast forest reserves made timber
one of the country's most
important industries throughout
the nineteenth century and up to
the present day.

The contrast between French and
British Canada is well illustrated
by these examples of nineteenth-
century architecture. Left: the
Parliament buildings in Ottawa,
built about 1878 in the Victorian
Gothic style. Right: the Basilica
of Notre-Dame-de-Quebec,
Quebec City, built about 1890.

The gold rush of the nineteenth century gave a tremendous stimulus to expansion in Canada, Australia, the United States and elsewhere, as townships grew out of mining settlements to develop economic lives of their own. During this period the world output of gold multiplied

about tenfold, and gold coins became regular British currency until 1914. The top picture shows the Cameron Claim in British Columbia; upper left is Rossland in the same province, and the upper right picture shows the gold escort at Roxburgh in New Zealand.

eager American individuals, but gradually, the frontier settled into probably the friendliest in the world. Once the Canadians no longer needed British military support, they were capable of acting as an independent country.

However it was long before the reality of Canadian independence was recognised in any legal theory. Up to the 1920s, Canada had no independent foreign relations with other countries; everything had to go through the British Foreign Office. The governors-general, up to 1931, were appointed on the advice of the monarch of the British, not the Canadian cabinet. Up to the Second World War, the governors-general were prestigious British citizens, not Canadians. In the formative years back in the nineteenth century, one governor in Canada, Lord Elgin, wrote that although his ministers were responsible to the legislature, 'no inducement on earth would prevail with me to acquiesce in any measure which seemed to me repugnant to public morals or Imperial interests'. Fortunately no such measure was ever presented to him.

The Canadian system reached its permanent framework with the British North America Act of 1867 which established it as a confederation of provinces. While the Canadian provinces have less independent power than the American states, the two countries had the common problem of colonising vast new territories to the west and a federal system was the obvious way to do this. Canadian 'manifest destiny' to colonise the west operated in much the same way and from much the same motives as the American one, although the Canadians tended to maintain better relations with the indigenous Indians and Eskimos.

The major Canadian difficulty was to establish a sense of national identity. Despite the vast size of Canadian territory, the overwhelming majority of the population grew up in a narrow strip running east to west across the north of the United States. Natural communications were more with American communities immediately to the south of them than to distant communities of fellow-Canadians. Thus such a city as Toronto has, by nature, much more to do with New York, Chicago or Detroit than with Vancouver, which is over 4,000 miles away.

The Gold Rush

The major stimulus for Canadian expansion westwards was the characteristic mid-nineteenth-century phenomenon of the 'gold rush'. This was also so in the United States, Australia, Russia and, in some measure, in South Africa. On the news that gold had been discovered in some remote, inhospitable territory, thousands of prospectors, eager to make fortunes, would rush out to stake their claims. A terminology passed into the English language from the slang of the 'diggers' with phrases such as 'panning out', 'lucky strike', 'wash-out', 'getting down to bedrock', 'stony broke' and so on. The discovery of gold on Vancouver island in 1858 attracted thousands of prospectors from many parts of the world, principally from California; this was the start of the province of British Columbia.

At the end of the century came another gold-rush to the remote north-western territory of the Yukon with the discovery of gold in the Klondike Valley. During this period the world output of gold multiplied about tenfold, thus providing economic lubrication for the industrialisation of Europe and the United States. Actual gold coins became, until 1914, the regular British currency. Some of the pioneer prospectors made fortunes but, in terms of the real interests of the 'gold rush' territories their real contribution was indirect. Townships grew up out of the mining settlements and these developed an economic life of their own.

Although the gold pioneers started new individual communities and, also, the fur traders travelled thousands of miles across Canada by sledge and canoe, the enormous Canadian land areas could not really be integrated into a single country until there was a railway. Like Kenya in Africa, Canada as a political entity was largely the creation of a railway. From the beginning of the confederation there had been a plan to build a railway to cement Canadian unity. The problem was that it would have to cross the Rocky Mountains and pass through something like 1,000 miles of territory north of Lake Superior which no white man had ever examined. For years the Canadians hesitated over a project which might prove ruinous. Eventually, however, the Canadian-Pacific railway was started by Scott in 1880 and completed in the unexpectedly short period of five years, the technical difficulties having turned out to be much less than had been anticipated.

The regular trans-Canadian rail services began in 1886 and thus opened up the rich virgin lands of Manitoba, Saskatchewan and Alberta to agriculture, just as the Dakotas and Minnesota were being opened up in the United States immediately to the south. Immigrants could stake out huge land claims and make them golden with wheat. In terms of majority numbers they were British (especially Scottish) and American, but there were also significant numbers of Germans and, in the far west, of Japanese, Chinese and (east) Indians. Almost no French came, however.

The main commercial centre of the Canadian west, Winnipeg, blossomed from a fur trading post into a major city. The confederal system was capable of absorbing politically the gigantic new provinces that were being carved out, although far into the twentieth century the relatively isolated Canadian western provinces had their own idiosyncratic political peculiarities, including a strong social credit movement.

Australia

The colonisation of Australia and New Zealand developed on much the same lines, politically, as that of Canada, although the Australian colonies—later called states—were closer to the American than the Canadian model in the amount of power they were allowed.

That Australia should ultimately become a new nation was a matter of deliberate planning by a group of imperialist idealists in London. The leading personality among them was Edward Gibbon Wakefield, who might have become an important British politician had he not been gaoled for abducting a young heiress. The episode ruined Wakefield's chances in British politics and he turned, instead, to agitating, writing and organising, largely behind the scenes, to establish new British settlements in Australia. Wakefield took it for granted that the whole land of Australia belonged to the British crown and the chief problem, in his view, was to fix the right price at which it could be sold to would-be colonisers. Too high a price, obviously, would discourage them and make settlement impossible. Too low a price would encourage sloppiness and inefficiency. The correct balance, Wakefield believed, was to fix prices at such a level that the indigent immigrant could hope, after two or three years as a hired labourer, to save enough money to buy his own land. During his period as an employee he would adapt himself to the colonial life; being forced to save money would make him a thrifty, sober citizen.

On the whole, Wakefield's ideas worked well, and by the mid-nineteenth century, the Australian colonies, although widely scattered, had taken root as the beginnings of a new nation. To the original settlement of Sydney in New South Wales were added Perth in western Australia, in 1829, Adelaide (a brilliant example of town planning) in South Australia in 1830, and Melborne in Victoria in 1835. Although empty land existed in the most bountiful profusion, the majority of Australians from the beginning preferred to settle in and around the new cities, a characteristic which has continued. This was mainly because much of the Australian space, especially in the north, was hot, arid and often dangerous. The original settlers of New South Wales were literally shut in on the coastal plain because the Blue Mountains to the west appeared to be impassable–early explorers in them simply got lost. However an expedition in 1811 found a route through them and pioneer squatters soon followed.

Although only a small minority of Australians actually engaged in exploration, the squatters, who staked out claims as big and bigger than whole English countries, were the first to acquire a characteristically 'Australian' national character. They were tough, silent and lonely and lacked the freneticism which made many Americans in comparable conditions pile up larger and larger fortunes beyond any reasonable family need. Their fortunes were built on sheep; the experiments carried out near Sydney by John Macarthur in the early nineteenth century with sheep imported from England and Spain produced a new breed which yielded more and better wool than any other in the world. By 1831 Australia was exporting two and a half million pounds of wool annually and this went on to revolutionise the European clothing industry.

However, as in western Canada, it was gold which accelerated Australia's growth. From 1851 fabulously rich goldfields were found in New South Wales, Victoria and Western Australia and immigrants poured in to exploit them. They came from all parts of the world, including America, and this further contributed to an Australian national character separate to that of Britain. Between 1850 and 1860 the Australian population leaped up from 405,000 to 1,146,000. Despite a certain amount of disorder in the goldfields, including one armed rebellion against the government which ended in a pitched battle, the new population was on the whole quite easily absorbed.

A major problem by the mid-nineteenth century was a gross imbalance of the sexes. The squatters in the interior, during the pioneering period, were mostly single men as were most of the gold prospectors. More or less by accident Caroline Chisholm, a British army officer's wife, found herself drawn into providing much of the solution towards it. She was shocked that many girls arriving from Britain were tempted away from chastity by the high rewards available for prostitution in the special Australian conditions. So she founded a hostel for them at Sydney where she chaperoned them carefully and married them off to decent husbands. From this she took to taking whole parties of girls 'up country' to seek out and marry sheep farmers. Then she returned home to England and solicited the help of such rich philanthropists as Lord Shaftesbury and Sydney Herbert to found the Family Colonisation Society. This, by means of loans, encouraged whole families to go to Australia, instead of single men, and also sent out women who had been left behind by their husbands. Mrs Chisholm is reckoned to have settled at least 15,000 immigrants, and her society ended up with a cash profit because its clients faithfully repaid their loans.

Politically, the new Australians gave the world the gifts of the secret electoral ballot. This procedure, which, during the latter part of the nineteenth century, was often actually termed the 'Australian ballot', entailed a voter marking a paper, without his name on it, in a private booth instead of having to announce his choice publicly with the danger of intimidation. The colony of Victoria, which was broken off from New South Wales in 1850 to form a separate administration, adopted it in 1856 and New South Wales almost immediately followed suit. Soon all the Australian colonies did so and then virtually all the world–the 'Australian system' by the mid-twentieth century was, at least formally, the normal method everywhere.

The secret ballot reflected a radicalism in Australian society which had been brought over direct from the trade unions and the Chartist movement back home in Britain. To an American in this period, 'equality' meant primarily equality of opportunity; an able or a lucky man could make a fortune, but it was not particularly society's concern to look after those who failed. Every man must make his own way. Australia, especially in the cities, developed a more socialistic outlook. Trade unionism in Australia established a Labour Party which came to power while the Labour Party in Britain was still a struggling minority.

Another aspect of this was the rigid 'white Australian' policy, which until 1966 rigorously excluded non-European immigrants. The reasoning behind this was the desire to establish a homogenous population: many Chinese and some Indians had come in during the gold rush period, and radical Australians feared they would be used as cheap labour in the interests of capitalists rather than of society at large. While 'white Australia' slowed up the development of the country, particularly the sugar industry in the tropical north, it did explode myths which existed elsewhere until well into the twentieth century that it was peculiarly dangerous for Europeans to live in a hot climate. The Australians were pioneers of the cult of the beach and the sun tan.

The Australian colonies steadily acquired constitutions which made them self-governing in a similar manner to Canada. Then in 1901 the colonies federated together to form the 'Commonwealth of Australia'. This was closer to the American model than to the Canadian in that the colonies, renamed states, retained a measure of organic independence instead of holding merely delegated powers.

New Zealand

Australia in the nineteenth century was often a rough, raucus country with a high crime rate, and good manners tended to be

Caroline Chisholm, known as 'the Emigrants Friend'. Mrs Chisholm, with the aid of rich philanthropists in Britain, founded the Family Colonisation Society, which helped and encouraged whole families to go to Australia, where previously men had gone alone. She also started a hostel for single girls arriving from England, and steered them away from the perils of prostitution by marrying them off to respectable sheep farmers.

Right: Edward Gibbon Wakefield, whose idealistic and influential views of systematic colonisation led to the foundation in 1834 of the South Australian Association and the establishment of the South Australian colony. He was also prominent in Canadian affairs for a time, accompanying Lord Durham as an adviser in 1838.

'The Golden Fleece', a painting by Tom Roberts. Many Australian fortunes were built on sheep farming – by 1831 the annual export had reached two and a half million pounds.

considered effete. New Zealand, 1,000 miles from Australia across the stormy Tasman Sea, was a gentler place, which grew up quite separately although, again, Wakefield was an influence behind the scenes.

The impetus for settlement in New Zealand, which was not fully annexed by the British crown until 1840, came largely from missionaries who wanted to convert the 100,000 Maori inhabitants to Christianity. In doing so, some of the missionaries made personal fortunes by developing their own land holdings but their motives, on the whole, were genuinely religious. The major figure among them was Bishop George Augustus Selwyn, who, often on foot and alone, made pioneering journeys from community to community to set up the Anglican Church. After a period of strain, and some fighting, the settlers, who included many Scots, came to terms with Maoris and race relations in New Zealand have since been generally good.

The New Zealand colonisers gradually developed a prosperous agriculture which relied upon the British market at the other side of the globe. Although they acquired self-governing constitutions, they remained the most loyal to Britain of all overseas emigrants. Indeed cynics dismissed them as an outlying British farm. By the latter part of the twentieth century, the abolition of the British monarchy was becoming a real possibility in both Canada and Australia, but the New Zealanders still completely accepted it.

India

Simultaneously with starting the new settler-societies in Canada, Australia and New Zealand, the British were proceeding vigorously towards the take-over of India. Wellesley's victories in the Napoleonic period had made Britain the paramount power in India, and from this base the local British officials on the spot proceeded to conquer the whole sub-continent, either subjecting it directly to their own rule or turning independent princes into vassals. Their military forces were mainly Indian. All this was against the wishes of the East India Company in London, which wanted profitable trade rather than conquest. Really there was a power-vacuum in India which the British, through military and administrative skill, were the best qualified to fill.

The only serious rival was the Sikh kingdom in the Punjab under an able monarch, Ranjit Singh. The Sikhs, bearded and militant, were primarily a religious group with an approximately similar relationship to orthodox Hinduism as that of Protestantism to Roman Catholicism. They rejected the Hindu caste system, militantly proselytised and taught virtues of self-defence and self-help. They were motivated by powerful nationalist feelings as well as a traditional love of conquest, and their ambition was to sweep the British out of India and become the paramount power in the sub-continent. The British defeated them in two wars between 1845 and 1849 and annexed the whole Punjab as British territory. Thereafter, although the Sikhs were often troublesome to British rulers, many individual Sikhs became the closest props of the British regime. They made excellent soldiers and the British found it easy to respect their religion.

The British also swept westwards to capture Sind – the commander Sir Charles Napier sent a message back: 'Peccavi', the Latin for 'I have sinned'. This was more than just a pun because he well knew that his aggressive policy was against East India Company policy. Three wars were conducted against Burma, which did not seem to appreciate the forces it was up against; one Burmese monarch provided his forces with a set of golden chains with which they were to bind the British governor-general. Finally in 1886, after wars which had lasted intermittently for sixty years, the British annexed Burma to India.

Charles Napier, soldier and statesman, who was responsible for the capture of Sind (now a region of Pakistan). In 1843 Napier won the brilliant victory of Miani, and later in the same year went on to destroy the army of the emirs at the battle of Hyderabad.

China

Next door to India lay the even greater prize of China. The British East India Company made far more profit out of China than ever it did out of India and, as the nineteenth century, so victorious for Britain, rolled on, the after-dinner talk of ambitious officials sometimes meandered to the possibility of annexing the Chinese Empire to the British crown. However, the particular set of conditions which had favoured the British conquest of India did not exist in China. The ancient imperial regime, although decayed, still provided China with a firm administrative framework which commanded the loyalty of the people. The Chinese government had an antiquity and an appeal to tradition which no authority in India had. The Chinese regarded their country as the centre of the world and held all outsiders to be barbarians. Then, also, other powers would not have allowed the British to seize China. The Russians, the French, the Americans, the Germans and, ultimately, the Japanese were all deeply interested.

However, there were bound to be clashes between the conservative Chinese and the zestful, aggressive Europeans, with

Britain in the lead. The first major incident occurred when the Chinese attempted to eliminate the opium trade in which British merchants were closely involved. By selling opium to the Chinese, the British financed profitable purchases of tea and silks. When, in 1842, the Chinese began physically interfering with ships carrying opium, the British, in alliance with other European powers, declared war.

Opium, as a narcotic, is about as dangerous as alcohol; that is it is capable of ruining a man, and is therefore highly dangerous, though many users get only pleasure out of it. Whether or not the Opium War against China is regarded as a supreme British infamy depends, really, upon one's attitude to narcotics. The Chinese, with their aged junks and ill-equipped army, had no chance against modern European forces, and the result of the war was to force Imperial China to throw its whole territory open for unrestricted trade and, in addition, to cede Hong-Kong island to the British and to allow sovereign foreign enclaves to be set up in five of its principal cities, including the capital of Peking. Inside these areas the Chinese had no legal jurisdiction at all. In the course of a further war, in 1860, an Anglo-French expedition occupied Peking, burned the emperor's summer palace and forced further concessions.

Stamford Raffles and Singapore

In a rather more peaceful manner, the British were also establishing themselves in Malaya and the East Indies, areas where the Dutch had been the European pioneers. The primary motive, as always, was trade, but also this area was one of the first in which the idealism, characteristic of some later British imperialism, became evident. The leading personality was Stamford Raffles, a young clerk of the East India Company who, when he was not suffering from blinding migraine, worked at his job with fanatical enthusiasm.

Raffles took unusual pains to get to know the subject peoples and thought that British rule should advance what he regarded as civilisation. In particular, he was energetic at suppressing slavery. When he was twenty-four he joined the East India Company office at Penang, Malaya. He studied the country and decided that British rule could bring it prosperity and happiness. When the company proposed to evacuate Malacca, which had been seized from the Dutch in the Napoleonic wars, Raffles wrote a passionate—and successful—memorandum of protest to London.

He was made Governor of Java during its temporary occupation by the British in the same wars, before it was returned to the Dutch, and deliberately set about trying to improve administrative standards. Finally, when the Congress of Vienna gave the Dutch back their Far Eastern interests, Raffles in 1819 leased from the Sultan of Penang a piece of land at the south of the Malayan peninsula and raised the British flag over it. This was the start of Singapore which, with enormous Chinese immigration, was to grow into the major port of the area. 'But for my Malay studies,' wrote Raffles, I should hardly have known that such a place existed; not only the European but also the Indian world was ignorant of it.' Raffles ran the new settlement at Singapore for only nine months before, at the age of forty-three, he retired to England because of ill-health and soon afterwards died (though not before he had been prominent in founding London Zoo, of which he was the first president).

In the hey-day of British imperialistic propaganda it became the fashion to over-romanticise Raffles. Certainly he made no personal profit from his imperialism. On his return to England the East India Company presented him with a bill for £20,000 which, is alleged, he had overspent in the work of government. The founding of Singapore was one of the greatest individual achievements in British history. Yet Raffles's conviction that direct British rule was essential for the welfare of technologically backward countries was probably less than completely healthy because it pioneered the later concept of 'the white man's burden' and thus much hypocrisy, both conscious and unconscious.

The urge to reform

The same kind of idea was growing up in India, in the wake of British conquest. In the first two generations of British power in India there was little ambition beyond prosecuting trade, suppressing disorder and ensuring British dominance. Christian missionaries, for example, had been excluded on the ground that they might cause disorder among the population by interfering with their beliefs—it took a political battle which lasted for years in London before the evangelical organisations managed to get that policy changed. But in the 1820s, with the emergence of a class of British civil servants who were administrators rather than soldiers or businessmen, this attitude changed. There grew up a positive ambition to 'improve' India and to eliminate social customs which were considered undesirable.

The prime activity was the suppression of 'suttee', an upper-class Hindu custom by which a widow was supposed to cremate herself on her husband's funeral pyre. If she failed to do this voluntarily, she was liable to be thrown on it forcibly. This practice was not surprisingly repugnant to the British, who knew little about Hindu theology. It was also repugnant to a Hindu reform group led by Ram Mohan Roy, a newspaper editor and philosopher who had visited Europe. Roy, the forerunner of the type of Indian intellectuals who were in the twentieth century to lead India to independence, joined the British in helping to suppress suttee, and this was largely achieved, although up to the present day there are still occasional instances of it being performed voluntarily. Told by Brahmins that suttee should be allowed to continue because it was a national custom, Napier, the conqueror of Sind, replied that the British also had national customs among them: 'that when men burn women alive we hang them'. He said suttee could continue if there could be a row of gibbets beside the funeral pyre on which the participants were hanged.

The suttee controversy, however, was only a fringe affair compared with a central idea that grew up of educating all India into becoming a second Britain. At its most extravagant it was expressed by the Whig politician, historian and poet Thomas Macauley, who served four years in India as a member of the governor-general's board of control. Under Macaulay's influence, it was laid down that higher education in India should be run on a British pattern, including Latin and Greek, and with the English language the medium of instruction.

In a speech in the House of Commons in London in 1835, Macaulay put forward the audacious ambition of producing a race of Indians who would be:

'Indian in blood and colour, but English in taste, opinions, morals and intellect . . . No nation can be perfectly well governed till it is competent to govern itself. It may be that the public mind of India may expand under our system till it has outgrown that system . . . that by good government we educate our subjects into a capacity for better government, so that they may demand European institutions.

'Whether such a day will ever come I do not know. Whenever it comes, it will be the proudest day of English history.'

The British Empire was not yet territorially complete but in those words of Macaulay were expressed the over-ambitious spirit that filled it in its prime. Men were really beginning to believe that a country off north-west Europe was capable of imposing its will and institutions on a sub-continent at the other side of the world.

View of the port of Canton, by an unknown artist. The British East India Company gained a firm foothold at Canton in the late seventeenth century, and the French and Dutch also established factories there in 1725 and 1762. From this time the city became by Imperial decree the only port for foreign trade, and the restrictive system by which the traders were forced to deal only with a small group of Chinese merchants caused increasing friction, ultimately leading to the Opium Wars.

Skinner's Horse performing a cavalry exercise (tent pegging), a painting by J. R. Giratkin, 1840. James Skinner, a British soldier who joined Lord Lake during the Mahratta war, formed a cavalry regiment which became the most famous of its time in India.

Right: *the siege of Gibraltar, a painting by G. Carter. This much sought-after stronghold in the Mediterranean has been the site of countless sieges since the Moors built their castle there in the eighth century. The British have maintained possession since 1704, though there were several attempts on the part of the Spanish to reclaim it by force. The most important was the siege of 1778–83, the subject of the illustration.*

*The Treaty of Nanking, which ended the Opium War of 1841–42,
forced the Chinese to open their entire territory to unrestricted trade, and
furthermore gave Britain the prize of Hong Kong island, destined to
become her greatest commercial base in the Far East.*

*A battle during the Sikh wars. The Sikh kingdom in the Punjab,
ruled by Ranjit Singh, was almost the only remaining obstacle to the
complete British take-over of India in the mid-nineteenth century. The
Sikhs were, however, eventually defeated in 1849, and the whole of the
Punjab annexed as British territory.*

Stamford Raffles, the founder of Singapore. Singapore, which was to grow into the major port of the area, began with a small strip of land leased by Raffles from the Sultan of Penang in 1819. Raffles could be said to epitomise British idealistic imperialism: when a clerk with the East India Company in Malaya he took great pains to study and get to know the people, and became convinced that British rule would bring them prosperity and advance their civilisation.

Below: the earliest known photograph of Singapore.

The 'Great White Queen'

Queen Victoria, symbol of imperial pride, ascended the throne at the age of eighteen, and reigned for sixty-four years. At the end of the Victorian era the British Empire itself had extended to cover a quarter of the world's land surface, and the whole world, with the exception of China, Japan, Siam, Persia and Ethiopia, was under white domination.

Victoria of Hanover, who in 1837, at the age of eighteen, ascended the throne of the world's richest country, was a passionate woman of small stature and homely looks. She had little imagination and distrusted innovation. Had she been an autocratic ruler, such as Catherine the Great of Russia, she would probably have been a disaster. However, although in the nineteenth century the powers of the British crown remained an active political factor, Victoria was hemmed in by parliamentary politicians, several of whom, such as Palmerston and Gladstone, she actively disliked.

In her middle life she passed through a period of genuine unpopularity and there was serious discussion of deposing her and inaugurating a British republic. But she had an extraordinarily long reign of sixty-three years and in her old age she became a venerated figure. It was at her golden and diamond jubilees of 1887 and 1897 that representatives of the empire were seen in procession in London and this was a powerful influence in making imperial pride an active force among the ordinary masses of British people.

Although Queen Victoria herself was almost wholly European in her outlook and never travelled outside Europe, one of the most important features of the Victorian era was the drawing together of the scattered human race into what can almost be considered as a single world community. This meant that educated members of every civilisation were conscious of the existence of other civilisations, and that disputes in any part of the globe were liable to become of world significance. There was nothing utopian about the world community of the Victorian era. It consisted of vigorous Europeans, utterly convinced that they were racially superior, sailing around the world in fast new steamships and attempting to impose their will on everybody else. The whole world, except for China, Japan, Siam, Persia and Ethiopia, fell under white domination (for this purpose, the Turkish and Russian empires are counted as Europeans). The British Empire was the chief force in this process.

The typical Victorian Englishman was an inextricable mixture of idealism, cupidity and pride. He distrusted foreigners but tended to enjoy being paternal towards races he regarded as his inferiors. Religion was often a powerful force in his life – Victorian Britain was soaked more thoroughly in Christian doctrine than at any time since the Middle Ages. Churches by the thousand were built at home, often in a pseudo-medieval style of architecture, and missionaries were sent out to convert peoples of other races. Missionary activity was, indeed, one of the mainsprings of the empire. The remarkable David Livingstone, for example, opened up central Africa to the British with primarily religious motivation.

There was a mystical side to British religion, typified by the high church Oxford Movement in the established Church of England. At its most extravagant it produced twelve 'apostles', including a member of parliament, who dressed up in lavish vestments and established a prosperous sect on the proposition that they had been divinely authorised to supervise all Christianity – they managed to establish sixty churches, each under an 'angel', in Britain, the United States and Germany.

More characteristic of the British religious impulse, however, was the evangelical movement, which distrusted frills and elaborate theology. The evangelicals were humanitarian, materialistic and puritanical. At their worst they were appallingly smug and hypocritical, and believed that business success was a divine reward for virtue. At their best, they encouraged honesty and good deeds. The evangelicals led the movement which abolished slavery in the British Empire. The creed of 'muscular Christianity', developed in the so-called 'public schools' in which most imperial administrators were educated,

The Khyber Pass, for centuries the trade and invasion route from central Asia, became a famous name in British military history in the period of the Afghan Wars.

had strong evangelical undertones, although it lacked the fanaticism of evangelicism proper.

At the start of the Victorian period, the British Empire consisted of coastal settlements in America, Africa and Australasia, plus many off-coast islands, and India. By the end of the Victorian period it had filled out into the interiors of the distant continents, thus covering a quarter of the world's land surface. Throughout the period, the Royal Navy dominated the world's sea routes; the army, in contrast, played only a subsidiary role in the empire-building process.

The British Indian Empire

The central fact in the Victorian empire was the entanglement in India. This was so not only because the sheer size of India made it important in itself, but also because the Indian involvement led to the large-scale acquisition of territories in Africa, the Middle East and Asia, with a view to protecting the route between Britain and India. The first new colony acquired in Victoria's reign, Aden, was occupied by the Bombay Presidency as a base for the suppression of piracy.

Until the twentieth century, British Indian administration had its own momentum and was unrelated to any grand design or long-term strategy drawn up in London. Vigorous men on the spot, many of them of high ability and lovers of India, enjoyed the work of government. For example three brothers,

Benjamin Disraeli, above and William Gladstone, right Queen
Victoria's two most influential prime ministers, the former
extravagantly adored by her, and the latter quite openly disliked.

Storming of the Delhi Gate, 1857. The causes of the Indian Mutiny have been a subject of much controversy; it has been interpreted as a nationalist uprising, the first stage in the movement for independence, while others see it as a purely local military affair. Whatever the causes, the effects were decisive and far-reaching: in 1858 the East India Company was abolished and rule assumed by the Crown; religious toleration was decreed, and Indians were for the first time admitted to the Civil Service, albeit in subordinate positions.

Left: *miniatures of three of the leaders of the Indian Mutiny. 1. Nana Sahib, the ruler of Cawnpore, where the most savage massacre of the uprising took place. 2. Kir Singh, a Rajput nobleman. 3. Lakhsmi Bai, the Rani of Jhansi, a romantic figure who wore men's clothes and fought at the head of her troops.*

The Victoria Memorial, Calcutta.

John, Henry and George Lawrence were placed in charge of the pacification and administration of the Punjab after the overthrow of the Sikh kingdom there. They had absolute power, unbound by any regulations, and they acted quickly and successfully to establish a settled government. One of their subordinates, John Nicholson, was deified as 'Nikkul Seyn' by a Hindu sect. Another, long afterwards, recalled: 'What days those were! How Henry Lawrence would send us off to great distances, Edwardes to Bunnoo, Nicholson to Peshawar, Abbott to Hazara, Lumsden somewhere else, etc., giving us a tract of country as big as half England, and giving us no more helpful directions than these, "Settle the country; make the people happy; and take care there are no rows!"'

Calcutta, the capital of British India, was growing from a trading settlement into one of the major cities of the world. Here administration was more bureaucratic than out in the newly-acquired Punjab. The governor-general from 1848 to 1856, the tenth Earl of Dalhousie, was a Scottish aristocrat of radical inclination. He was appointed at the age of thirty-six. He built the first railways in Asia and gave India a 4,000 mile telegraph system which was a more complete service than that which existed in Britain at the time. Working at high speed, he constantly annexed small Indian states and planned an elaborate education system.

The Indian mutiny

Hardly had Dalhousie retired from office than India blew up in revolt. It has sometimes been held that the rapid pace of Dalhousie's administration had provoked this, but in fact the evidence points more to local grievances in the Bengal army as the cause of the mutiny of 1857, rather than any generalised political sentiment. The soldiers' pay was in arrears, and they were under the impression that they were to be converted forcibly to Christianity. The breaking point, apparently, was the issue of greasy cartridges which a soldier had to bite open before using. Hindu soldiers believed that the grease came from cows, their sacred animals, and the Moslems believed it came from pigs, which they regard as unclean.

After months of mild disorder, during which troops at Dumdum refused to obey orders, the mutiny flared up in full force at Meerut on a hot Sunday evening. Three regiments shot their British officers and marched off to Delhi, where they joined forces with the local Indian garrison and proclaimed their allegiance to Bahadur Shah, the last of the Moghul emperors, a blind old man of eighty-two. It was a measure of the thinness of British power that the Delhi arsenal, the biggest in northern India, had only two British officers and three British sergeants among its guard.

Other outbreaks followed and for two months there was serious doubt as to whether British power could last in India. The weakness of the mutineers, however, lay in their lack of coherent leadership, and despite such Indian princes as Nana Sahib and the glamorous twenty-year-old Rani of Jhansi, who put on men's clothes and fought at the head of her troops, deliberately planning to subvert the army, there was no comprehensive long-term plan. The mass of the Indian population did not appear to care too much whether the mutineers or the British won. The Madras and Bombay presidencies remained quiet.

The fighting was bitter in the extreme, with both sides murdering prisoners. The British were particularly horrified when their wives and children were cut down. On both sides, also, there was much individual heroism. The British took immense pride in the siege of the residency at Lucknow where, for nearly three months, the white garrison held out against superior forces. The commander, Henry Lawrence, died of wounds early in the siege, but the memory of his outstanding power of leadership helped to maintain the garrison's morale. From the siege of 1857 until the moment of Indian independence ninety years later, a Union Jack flew permanently by night and day over the Lucknow residency as a memorial to Lawrence and his men. The last flag at Lucknow was eventually hauled down in an emotional ceremony and sent off to King George VI to be stored at Windsor Castle.

Lucknow was militarily important because it tied down large numbers of the rebels. However, the crucial point in the war was Delhi, which most Indians still regarded as their national capital. So long as Bahadur Shah claimed his prerogatives as emperor (or appeared to claim them – he did not really understand what was going on), the rebels had strong pretensions to legitimacy and there could be no certainty about how the Indian princes would go. But the recently pacified Punjab remained loyal and John Lawrence was able to strip it of forces to march against Delhi. Some 5,000 British and Sikhs attacked a rebel occupation force of 30,000 and, after six days of extremely bloody fighting, succeeded in achieving a surrender. A quarter of the British attacking force was killed, including its commander, Nikkul Seyn. The emperor was sent off to exile in Rangoon and his two sons, the last of his dynasty, were shot out of hand on the pretext that they were attempting to escape.

By the autumn of 1857, with Delhi recaptured and Lucknow relieved, the mutiny had ceased to be really dangerous to the British, but it took a further two years before the last of the rebel soldiers were captured. It was often an atrocious operation, the British regarding their opponents as monsters who had slaughtered white women and children. Prisoners were fortunate if they were shot or hanged. With the knowledge, if not the connivance, of the highest British authorities, many rebels were tortured to death – one device being to sew them up in an animal skin and then put them out into the sun to die, while others were fired from cannons.

Strengthening rule

One consequence of the mutiny was to fasten British rule upon India more closely than ever before. East India Company rule, which, especially since the company had lost its monopoly trading rights in 1833, had become hardly more than a fiction, was abolished and instead India was brought directly under the British crown. The governor-general was given the extra title of viceroy, to stress that he was the direct representative of the monarch. In 1876 the romantically minded prime minister, Benjamin Disraeli, added the title of 'Empress of India' to Queen Victoria's designations.

At the same time, however, the British became fundamentally more cautious in their approach to the Indians. The spate of annexations of Indian states ceased and, instead, the Indian princes were supported on their thrones, encouraged to make big incomes and flattered by being given decorations, salutes and guns. Some of the Indian rajahs became the richest men in the world by taxing their subjects. The condition was that they accepted a measure of 'advice' from British political officers, drawn mostly from the army, who were stationed at their courts. The princely rulers were not supposed to communicate with each other, except through the British authorities, and were allowed to have no relationship with any foreign power.

India, as it ossified in the 1860s, consisted in land area half of 'British India', ruled directly, and half of princely India. The British aim was to make the princes a buttress of their own power but, in the following century, the rise of middle-class nationalism changed the relationship so that the British found themselves buttressing the princes. A crucial factor, in the nineteenth century, was that the princely states did not form a

Top: *view of Government House, Calcutta, an aquatint by J. B. Fraser. The design was based on that of Kedleston Hall, Derbyshire. Calcutta, capital of British India, grew rapidly from a trading settlement into one of the major cities of the world.*

Above: *the massacre at Cawnpore, the most notorious episode in the Indian mutiny, when hundreds of women and children were hacked to death, and their bodies thrown down a well.*

Frederick Lugard, who brought the kingdom of Buganda under the control of the British East Africa Company, was instrumental in persuading the British government to annex Uganda, and later, when in service with the Royal Niger Company, transformed Nigeria from a small settlement into the largest coastal colony in Africa.

Right: the English explorer John Hanning Speke, whose conviction that the source of the Nile lay in Lake Victoria became the subject of a prolonged and acrimonious public debate. Speke died in 1864, having shot himself – possibly accidentally – before his theory was proved correct by subsequent explorations.

Top: 'Elephants in the Shallows of the Shire River – the steam launch firing', by Thomas Baines. Baines was appointed artist to Livingstone's Zambezi expedition at the recommendation of the Royal Geographical Society. The launch is the Ma-Robert, which accompanied the expedition.

Above: 'T. Baines and G. Humphrey killing an alligator', by Thomas Baines. In March 1855 Baines was appointed artist and storekeeper to the North Australian expedition, the leader being A. C. Gregory, later surveyor-general of Queensland. Mr Humphrey was the second overseer on this expedition.

continuous land mass but were dotted about separately as islands within British territory. The princely realms ranged from Hyderabad, which was roughly the size of Italy, down to Nongliwai, which was just a hillside in Assam.

Caution, also, meant a slowing up, indeed an abandonment, of Macaulay's ambitious design to turn Indians into Englishmen, and this, by the twentieth century, had developed into a tendency to automatically regard even educated Indians as inferiors. Social and sexual intercourse between British and Indians dwindled away, the British spending their off-duty hours in their private clubs and messes. This was partly because Indians had badly frightened the British, and there was now a tendency to regard them as 'inscrutable' and dangerous.

The process of isolation of British and Indians from each other was accentuated by the arrival of ever-larger numbers of British wives. Younger British officials and officers were expected to be bachelors, but most mature men had wives. It became social and professional death for a British man to marry an Indian girl. Such illicit relationships as did take place were kept quiet, and the Eurasian community, which was the result of the first contacts between British and Indians, tended to become self-propagating, with relatively little infusion of fresh British blood. However, the Eurasians far out-numbered the pure British in India; their educational standard was not high but English was their mother tongue and they were literate. They were, in this period, intensely pro-British and referred to the England they had never seen as 'home'. The pure British treated them patronisingly, regarding them as a subsidiary support for their rule, and reserved jobs for them in the customs and on the railways.

The new crown administration entailed the foundation of the Indian Civil Service which, in sheer intellectual calibre, was one of the best bureaucracies ever to have existed anywhere. It was recruited from the cream of Oxford and Cambridge graduates: because their pay, pensions and holidays in India were more liberal, many able young men preferred the Indian service to that at home in Britain. The Indian Army too, attracted British officers of high calibre, because in India they could live on their pay, whereas in the exclusive social atmosphere of the British Army most officers required a private fortune in order to exist. The Indian Army, the successor to the old presidency armies of the East India Company, was allowed no artillery because of the mutiny, and it was generally stationed on the frontiers far away from its home recruiting areas; also, at Indian expense, it was used for the further expansion of the British Empire. The internal garrisons in India were mostly purely British regiments, paid for from Indian revenues.

By the end of the Victorian era, the British Indian Empire had settled into an apparently immutable pattern. It seemed utterly normal that young British men, who had been carefully educated in Latin and Greek, should set off across the world to govern an alien sub-continent, and that a British politician should, as viceroy, command an empire second in size only to China.

The actual numbers of British involved in governing India were extremely small – the Indian Civil Service had only 1,200 members – but an entire way of life was evolved. In the hot summer months the executive moved from Calcutta to the mountain station of Simla, where a complete Victorian town was built, with a remarkably ugly viceregal palace in Scottish baronial style. Every sizeable Indian town had its 'cantonment', a sort of segregated suburb in which the British formed a self-contained community run on rigidly hierarchical principles. The memory of the mutiny was still fresh and many a cantonment had its local ghost story stemming from a victim of that event.

The throne presented to the queen by the Maharaja of Travancore, made about 1840 and displayed at the Great Exhibition of 1851.

Right: *the proclamation of Queen Victoria as Empress of India at Delhi, 1877. Victoria never visited India, but she nevertheless took great pride in her new subject peoples, and acquired a taste for Indian objects, and even Indian food.*

About the only area of administration in which Indians achieved some prominence was the law. Some, such as the young Mohandas Gandhi, travelled to London to qualify as barristers at the inns of court and there were instances of Indians being appointed judges even in the high Victorian era. When, however, a Liberal viceroy, Lord Ripon, proposed to make British residents, as well as Indians, liable to be tried before Indian judges, there was such an outcry that he was forced to abandon the idea. As one retired official, who had been foreign secretary to the government of India put it, the proposal outraged 'the cherished conviction which was shared by every Englishman in India, from the highest to the lowest, by the planter's assistant in his lowly bungalow and by the editor in the full light of the presidency town–from those to the Chief Commissioner in an important province and to the viceroy on his throne–the conviction in every man that he belongs to a race whom God has destined to govern and subdue'.

While a majestic machine of British administration was growing in India, the rest of the British Empire was proliferating outwards.

'His Highness Rajah Booke'

One of the more romantic figures in this period was James Brooke, who started his career by fighting for the British Indian administration in the first Burmese war. Then he inherited a small fortune and used it to buy and equip a ship in which he intended to be an independent merchant-adventurer in the East Indies. He assisted a local sultan in the northern part of the island of Borneo to put down a rebellion and, as a reward, was in 1841 made rajah of Sarawak, which had been part of the sultan's territory. Brooke, who was interested in power rather than money, accepted this independent little principality and ran it on his own lines. He believed that the normal British colonial pattern of officials standing aloof from the local population was a mistake, and he identified himself with his subjects as if he were a native ruler–he appointed a council of two British and three local chiefs to advise him. Over a period of forty years, 'His Highness Rajah Brooke' extended Sarawak until it had become the largest territory in northern Borneo.

Brooke's establishment of himself as an independent sovereign was an achievement unique in British imperial history and, indeed, it ran counter to the British legal principle that territories acquired by British subjects should come under the British crown. In 1888, under the threat of a Royal Navy expedition being sent, his nephew, who had succeeded him, agreed to conduct his foreign relations through Britain and to make no further territorial gains without London consent. Three generations of the Brooke family ruled in Sarawak until its occupation by Japan in the Second World War. 'I work like a galley slave,' wrote the first rajah. 'I fight like a common soldier, the poorest man in England might grumble at my diet, luxuries I have none, necessities are often deficient. I am separated from civilised life and educated men . . . Could money tempt a man to this?'

Malaya

From their base at Singapore, the British penetrated steadily northwards into Malaya, the process being a peaceful one of

During the hot summer months the executive of the British government of India moved to the mountain-station of Simla above, *where a complete Victorian town was built, with a viceregal palace in Scottish baronial style and,* above right, *a church which would not have looked out of place anywhere in the British Isles.*

James Brooke who, having helped a sultan in Borneo to put down a rebellion, was made rajah of Sarawak as a reward. He ran the principality on his own lines—he disagreed with the British colonial pattern of aloof administration—devised a simple tax system and administered justice personally. Over a period of years he extended Sarawak to become the largest territory in northern Borneo.

View of Cape Town in the nineteenth century. It was here that van Riebeeck landed in 1652.

Malayan sultans accepting treaties which put them under British 'protection'. It was slow at first but speeded up with the introduction of the rubber industry in the 1870s. The Marquess of Salisbury, then secretary of state for India in the London government and a future prime minister, was an amateur scientist who had conceived the idea of collecting rubber seeds from South America and trying to find somewhere in the eastern British Empire where they could be planted successfully. The best soil for them turned out to be in Malaya, and a major rubber industry grew up which, with the invention of the motor car, turned out to be of central importance. Well into the mid-twentieth century, Malayan rubber was a major support for the pound sterling. The Malayans themselves were not enthusiastic about working in the rubber plantations, and immigrant the long run was to prove yet another cause for much inter-racial trouble.

Africa

The major expansion in the Victorian era was the opening up of the interior of Africa to European contact. At the start of Victoria's reign most of central Africa was a place of complete mystery to Europeans. It was marked *terra incognita* on the maps. Nobody knew the source of the Nile; no European had ever seen the Victoria Falls or Mount Kilimanjaro. Arab slave traders had long known their way around Africa – their Moslem faith had spread from east to west across the continent – but Europeans knew only the coasts.

For reasons connected with slavery, and later with its suppression, the British had established bases and trading settlements in West Africa, but there had been no attempt at colonisation save in the special case of Sierra Leone, which was the haven for freed slaves, and Gambia, which was an island trading

fort. The climate was, with reason, regarded as deadly for whites, with malaria, black-water fever and yellow fever often proving fatal. There were moments in the mid-nineteenth century when the whole administration of Sierra Leone seemed in danger of dying out.

In the south, the British had acquired Cape Colony from the Dutch in the Napoleonic wars and they held on to it because it controlled the Atlantic route to India. The original Dutch settlers – the Boers – disliked British administration and many of them trekked inland to form the republics of the Transvaal and Orange River. The British claimed that they were still under their suzerainty and this problem came to a climax in the Boer War at the end of Victoria's reign. Natal, to the north-east of Cape colony, attracted substantial numbers of British and Indian settlers and in 1856 was constituted a separate colony.

There were four reasons why the British expanded in Africa in the nineteenth century: a desire to guard the route to India; a determination to expand trade; religious zeal, and rivalry with other European powers.

The Suez Canal, opened in 1869, was a French enterprise but, obviously, it was crucial for the India route. The British from the start were the largest customers and in 1875 the British prime minister, Disraeli, bought control of it. To guard the Suez Canal it was necessary for the British to occupy Egypt, although until 1914 it remained formally a part of the Turkish Empire. To hold Egypt securely entailed occupying its hinterland, the Sudan. The Egyptian economy depended upon the Nile, and so when its source in Uganda was discovered, the country had to be occupied in order to protect the Nile. Then Kenya, the territory between Uganda and the east coast, had to be occupied lest the Germans or anybody else seized it and thus cut off the British in Uganda. To round this off, the island of Zanzibar, the ancient centre for Arab trade in East Africa, had to be brought under British protection.

British Somaliland was acquired because it had a coastline

dominating the Gulf of Aden through which British ships passed on their way to India. A similar process took place on the Arabian side. From their initial base at Aden the British brought under their 'protection' neighbouring shiekhdoms in the Persian Gulf and on the Trucial Coast, partly to suppress piracy and partly to prevent any other European power occupying them. Much later, of course, this became a major oil-producing area.

With steadily expanding industry at home, and a steadily rising standard of living, the British needed raw materials and outlets for their finished products. It was this that led them into the Gold Coast and into what became Nigeria. Coastal stations, such as Accra and Lagos, were annexed in order to trade in such goods as palm oil, which was needed for soap (in the Victorian era the British were for the first time becoming a clean nation) and cocoa.

Inevitably, the British became enmeshed in local politics and found themselves annexing more and more territory inland. In the huge territory of Nigeria this was largely accomplished by peaceful treaties, but in the Gold Coast the ancient Ashanti kingdom was obliterated by force. The French, who obtained the greater part of West Africa, operated in similar manner.

Missionary Exploration

The nineteenth century missionary spirit was linked to a determination to abolish slavery and the slave trade, which was based upon Zanzibar. This existed to some extent as a force in both East and West Africa – at one point there was an actual religious war in Uganda between Protestant and Catholic converts – but it was at its strongest in central Africa. If there was one Victorian folk-hero who stood out above all others it was the explorer-missionary David Livingstone. A devoutly religious medical doctor from Blantyre, Scotland, Livingstone had no particular skill as a preacher, and although he started his career in Africa nominally as a missionary he never really operated as one. He established no mission stations and made few, if any, converts.

He started off in southern Africa where the manner in which the Boers treated Africans aroused wrath. 'It is difficult,' he wrote, 'for a person in a civilised country to conceive that any body of men . . . should with one accord set out, after loading their own wives and children with caresses, and proceed to shoot down in cold blood men and women of a different colour.' The Boers claimed that Livingstone was making the Africans obstreperous and more or less drove him away, tearing up his books and stealing his medicines. Then Livingstone set off on a series of four journeys of exploration which added a million square miles to the map of Africa. On the first two he was nominally a missionary, but for the other two he was appointed a British 'consul', with formal powers to negotiate with the chiefs of African tribes – he liked to wear the cap of the consular uniform.

Between each journey, Livingstone returned to London where he lectured and became a major public hero, crowds flocking around him whenever he appeared in public. Although he could be autocratic in dealing with Africans, he loved them and insisted that they were human beings, an idea which was a novelty to some. He argued that they should be brought under British control in order to be civilised and converted to Christianity.

During his last journey across Africa, which began in 1865, Livingstone seemed to disappear altogether. He was ill, at various times, with rheumatic fever, pneumonia and dysentery, all of which he recorded in his journal. Sometimes on foot and sometimes carried by his African porters, he ranged backwards and forwards between Lakes Nyasa and Tanganyika in search of the source of the Nile. For years on end nobody outside knew what had happened to him. The *New York Herald* sent a reporter, Henry Stanley, to find him and, after months of searching, Stanley located him. On hearing the news that a white man had arrived, Livingstone rose from his hut, where he was resting, and went to the door. Stanley advanced slowly towards him, with crowds of Africans and Arabs watching.

'I would have run to him,' wrote Stanley, in perhaps the most famous newspaper dispatch ever printed, 'only I was a coward in the presence of such a mob – would have embraced him, only, he being an Englishman, I did not know how he would receive me; so I did what cowardice and false pride suggested was the best thing – walked deliberately to him, took off my hat, and said "Dr Livingstone, I presume?" '

Stanley, who himself became a significant explorer, surveying the Congo on behalf of the Belgian king, spent a year travelling with Livingstone and tried to persuade him to return home. But Livingstone, ill as he was, was determined to remain in Africa. In 1873, a year after Stanley had left him, Livingstone died at Chitambo in what is now Zambia. His personal servants Susi and Chumah displayed practical devotion by carrying Livingstone's body 1,500 miles to the coast – it took them nine months – and handing it over to the British consul. They also brought Livingstone's books, journals and maps. Two months later Susi and Chumah had a position of honour at Livingstone's funeral at Westminster Abbey, London.

This was a story of such romance that it fired British missionaries, especially Scottish ones, to follow up Livingstone's work in central Africa. With the setting up of missionary stations in what are now Malawi and Zambia these territories gradually became peacefully absorbed into the British Empire.

The scramble for land

The fourth motive for British penetration into Africa was rivalry with other European powers. While such British explorers as Burton and Speke, who succeeded where Livingstone had failed in discovering the source of the Nile, were prominent in mapping the continent, the French and the Germans were also active. The French spread across West Africa, southwards and eastwards from the Sahara Desert. Their mercenary force, the Foreign Legion, formed in 1835, established chains of fortified stations. When in 1898 a French advance party reached the Nile at Fashoda in the Sudan there was nearly another Anglo-French war.

The German Karl Peters pioneered the exploration of what became Kenya and Tanganyika. The newly united kingdom of Italy had its interests in Somaliland and ambitions to conquer Ethiopia. The Portuguese were active in their ancient colonies of Angela and Mozambique, with some ambition to unite them by occupying the area that became the Rhodesias. Spain had a toehold at Rio Muni in West Africa. In a spirit of competition, the British often formed new colonies not so much because they really wanted them but because they wanted to avoid any other European power occupying them.

In 1884 at an international conference in Berlin, the leading European powers coolly split up Africa into definite spheres of influence. The frontiers drawn up then are, in wide measure, still the frontiers of independent African states nearly a century later. Britain obtained Southern and most of East Africa together with the right to extend inland from its coastal colonies in the west. The French gained the bulk of West Africa, plus a piece of Somaliland. The Germans got Tanganyika, South-West Africa and the Cameroons, the Italians the bulk of Somaliland, while Leopold II of Belgium acquired the Congo as a personal estate, which he exploited with unusual vigour and harshness. The Portuguese and Spanish were left with their *status quo*. As a side-

Right: Punch *cartoon: 'the Rhodes Colossus'. Where Stamford Raffles may be said to epitomise the idealistic strain of British imperialism, Cecil Rhodes stands for another aspect – expansion for the sake of power. His most dramatic success was the formation of two new colonies, Northern Rhodesia and Southern Rhodesia, the land being acquired largely by means of straightforward swindles.*

Below: *Boer farmers on the Great Trek. The Boers had for some time disliked British rule in Cape Colony, and about 1836 they began their mass migration northwards to form the republics of Transvaal and the Orange River. However, the British government was not prepared to relinquish control over them, and the problem finally erupted in the Boer War of 1899– 1902.*

Right: *'Sons of the Blood', by S. Begg, a romanticised interpretation of British power in the Boer War. Although Great Britain won the war through sheer weight of numbers, the aftermath of bitterness against Britain continued to affect the political life of South Africa.*

The opening of the Suez canal in 1869. The canal was originally a French enterprise, but it was obviously crucial for the India route, and in 1875 Disraeli, then prime minister, bought a major shareholding from the Khedive Ismail of Egypt.

Isandhlwana. Zulu war, 1879, by C. E. Fripp. Expansion in South Africa was hindered for some time by the warlike Zulu people, who had already inflicted grave losses on the Boer trekkers. In 1878 the British launched an attack on the Zulus under chief Cetewayo, who had ignored an ultimatum that he submit to British rule. He was defeated the following year, but at the expense of many British lives.

The explorer and missionary David Livingstone, seen here with his daughter Agnes. Livingstone, a genuinely devout man who started his career as a missionary, in fact made few converts and established no mission stations. His ambition was larger – he hoped to abolish the slave trade, which appalled him, and open up central Africa to Christianity. His example began a tradition of missionary activity which resulted in large territories being peacefully absorbed into the British Empire.

deal in 1890, the British swapped the North Sea island of Heligoland for a German pledge to keep their hands off Uganda.

If Livingstone had introduced a definitely humanitarian strain into British colonialism, two other powerful personalities, Frederick Lugard and Cecil Rhodes, stand out as representing other strains in it in the Victorian era.

Frederick Lugard

Born at Madras in 1858, the son of an East India Company chaplain, Lugard failed the examination for the Indian Civil Service, but was commissioned in the British Army in India. Although he was keen on combat, Lugard was appointed a transport officer and it was in this capacity that he first visited Africa with a contingent from India fighting in Ceylon. Back in Lucknow he fell in love with an English girl. He was assigned as a transport officer to Burma and, while there, heard that his girl-friend had been hurt in a riding accident. He obtained leave and rushed to Lucknow to be at her side but, on his arrival, found that she had left for London. He bought a ticket on the next ship and set off in pursuit, only to find, when he finally caught up with her, that she had become engaged to marry somebody else.

Heartbroken, Lugard decided to abandon his settled career and instead seek adventure wherever he could. He later wrote in his diary: 'With fifty sovereigns in my belt, and with practically no outfit at all except my favourite little ·450 rifle, I got on board the first passing ship, as a second-class passenger, and sailed I knew not whither.'

The ship turned out to be going to Naples, and there Lugard tried to join the Italian army, which was fighting in Ethiopia. The Italians turned him down and he drifted towards East Africa, where he heard that a minor war was being waged against slave raiders near Lake Nyasa. He set off by canoe to join in the fighting and, working closely with missionaries, he took command of the forces of the Lakes Company, the British commercial concern which was opening up the area for trade, and drove out the slavers. The war won, he travelled home to England where he agitated for Nyasaland to be placed under British protection with himself as governor. However, although he made important friends in London, including Cecil Rhodes, he was dependent on the influence of others to get the protectorate declared, and he was not appointed governor.

He returned to Africa in the service of the East Africa Company, which was conducting trade with the sophisticated Uganda kingdom of Buganda and certainly wanted profitable trade rather than conquest. In conditions of rivalry with the French, of civil war, and with the kabaka (king) of Buganda persecuting his Christian subjects, Lugard used hired soldiers to win control of the territory. The company repudiated him and Lugard went back to England where he conducted a successful public campaign to persuade the government to annex Uganda on the ground that it was vital for the security of India. The prime minister, the Liberal W. E. Gladstone, was not enthusiastic about making new imperial acquisitions, but he capitulated in the face of the public opinion Lugard had aroused.

Of course Lugard was not really closely concerned about the safety of the route to India. His real motivation was that he found satisfaction in administering the affairs of Africans. Unlike Livingstone he was not particularly religious, but he was a born leader and a paternalistic humanitarian. Also he was a fervent patriot, believing that everything that was British was best, and he believed, too, in the code of honour of the Victorian 'English gentleman'.

Having brought Uganda into the empire, Lugard moved to the other side of Africa in the service of the Royal Niger Company. Partly with a view to eradicating slavery, partly to keep out the French and partly from sheer love of imperial expansion for its own sake, Lugard transformed Nigeria from a mere coastal settlement into the biggest coastal colony in Africa. He achieved this partly by treaty with the emirs and chiefs in the interior and partly by conquest over them with a local, mainly African army which he raised. He himself preferred conquest, as he felt there was an element of ambiguity, or even duplicity, in the peaceful treaties.

First as governor of northern Nigeria and then as governor-general of all Nigeria, Lugard worked out from scratch his methods of administration, which were to be widely imitated in the whole of British Africa. His leading idea was 'indirect rule', by which the British, so far as possible, preserved traditional African society and worked through the existing chiefs. This was quite different from the method of the neighbouring French which had the long-term objective of turning Africans into Frenchmen. In the early colonising period, however, 'indirect rule' was certainly an efficient method; later it became less effective because it gave no scope for the new African middle and professional classes which began to arise as a result of contacts with Europe.

To administer 'indirect rule', Lugard recruited British district officers, whom he preferred to have been educated at public schools. They should be incorruptible and have 'an almost passionate sense of fair play'. This, too, was to become characteristic of the British African service as a whole.

Lugard developed a doctrine of 'the mandate of civilisation' which justified the British taking over African territory. While he sought no personal enrichment, he insisted that the mineral and agricultural riches of Africa were the heritage not just of Africans but of mankind generally. He was supremely happy just governing and, in the end, he made up for the amorous disappointment of his youth by marrying Miss Flora Shaw, colonial correspondent of the London newspaper, *The Times*.

Cecil Rhodes

Cecil Rhodes, who was roughly Lugard's contemporary but died much younger, was an empire-builder of a more extreme type. Indeed at times he touched insanity, with his megalomaniac ideas that the Anglo-Saxon and German races should, between them, dominate the whole world. Son of an English clergyman, he early made a millionaire's fortune in the South African diamond mines. For years after that he kept returning to England to keep terms at Oxford University so that he could become a bachelor of arts – he cut an odd figure among the other undergraduates.

He was a lifelong bachelor, who undoubtedly had high powers of leadership. He used his politics to bolster his business interests and his businesses to bolster his political aims. As prime minister of Cape Colony, which as a white-settled territory had a wide measure of self-government, he fomented attacks on the Boer republics of the Transvaal (where the Rand diamond mines were) and the Orange Free State to the north with the intention of forcing them under full British control. This was one of the factors that led to the Boer War at the very end of Victoria's reign, though of course the war was not only Rhodes's fault. The Boers refused citizenship to immigrant British who arrived at the Rand and, under the fanatically traditionalist Paul Kruger of the Transvaal, conceived an ambition to drive the British out of South Africa altogether. The war was caused by intransigence on both sides and, although the British won militarily by sheer weight of numbers, the Boers later won politically.

Rhodes's most dramatic success was the formation of two new colonies, Northern Rhodesia and Southern Rhodesia, named after himself. He raised capital in the City of London to form a British South Africa Company and won some limited support from the British government. He sent agents northwards to negotiate a treaty with King Lobengula of the Matabele, which was a straightforward swindle. The king thought he was selling the company only the right to mine minerals, but in fact Rhodes's adventurers treated him as if he had signed away his entire country.

In 1890 the 'pioneer column' of settlers trekked northwards and named their first base 'Fort Salisbury' after the prime minister of the day—this being tactful flattery because it was none too certain that London would approve. This, from the start, was intended to be a colony of white settlement, like Canada or Australia, and not a 'civilising' programme like that of Lugard in Nigeria. Within two years, the Africans were at war with these people, whom they regarded as interpolaters.

The settlers called this a 'rebellion' and put it down, with Rhodes now personally in the lead. Even in the highest and most self-confident days of empire, there was some doubt in London about his methods. However, during Rhode's lifetime and for a long time afterwards the British South Africa Company made no profits although ultimately it did so on a vast scale, with the development of the copperbelt in Northern Rhodesia (now Zambia) in the 1930s.

Rhodes had a presentiment that he would die young and, whenever he felt depressed, he drafted a will by which his money was to be used to forward his ideas after his death. His first will, made when he was twenty-four, proposed to set up a secret society which would have the objects of spreading British power across the world and of getting the United States back into the empire. 'I contend,' he wrote at this time, 'that we are the first race in the world, and that the more of the world we inhabit, the better it is for the human race. I contend that every acre added to our territory provides for the birth of more of the English race, who otherwise would not be brought into existence. Added to which the absorption of the greater part of the world under our rule simply means the end of all wars.'

Rhodes died in 1902, at the age of forty-eight, at a moment when his reputation was tarnished by the Boer War. His final will was relatively moderate—he left his fortune of £4 million to found scholarships at Oxford for students from the colonies, the United States and Germany.

Clash of cultures

Livingstone, Lugard and Rhodes, between them, epitomised the varying qualities of the Victorian British Empire in Africa. Each, in his own way, was a man of imagination and extreme ambition. Perhaps Lugard was the most typical, because in moral quality he stood midway between the other two. But all the imagination and all the energy in the world would not have enabled them to expand British influence and power without the special conditions that existed at the time of the first encounters between technologically advanced Europeans and unsophisticated Africans.

Many Victorians had a vague idea that Africans were 'savages', but this was based upon incorrect information; in fact many of the African kingdoms and tribes were easily at the level of sophistication of late medieval Europe. However, like the medieval Europeans they had only the dimmest knowledge, if any, of the real shape of the world and of cultures other than their own. The first clash with the British was bound to be a debilitating shock and, indeed, the British did appear sometimes to be super-men to them. Also the British had better weapons, better skill in military organisation and the ability to call upon support from their homeland when serious conflict occurred. It is a fallacy to suppose that the British occupation of their African colonies was an entirely peaceful process: there were serious wars in Zululand, Ashanti, the Sudan, Uganda, Southern Rhodesia, Somaliland, and northern Nigeria, to name only a few.

In retrospect it is clear that the British Empire in Africa, like that in India, was a mere by-product of the first encounter of cultures at a different technological stage of development. Once the subject peoples had begun to absorb some of the technical skills of the British—and these were not particularly difficult to learn—the relationship automatically changed and the British imperial idea ceased to be viable. Probably the most important British influence in Africa was that which ended slavery which, apart from its inherent unpleasantness, is in all but the most primitive communities an economically unprogressive arrangement.

Egypt and the Sudan

The only African territory not yet discussed is Egypt, which was very much a special case. The black African colonies were, on the whole, acquired by the initiative of individuals on the spot rather than by settled London policy. Egypt, however, with its crucial strategic position, its sophisticated civilisation and its relationships with Turkey and France, represented a central factor in British foreign policy.

Napoleon Bonaparte, as a French revolutionary army commander, had been the first European to conquer Egypt, and from the scientists and archaeologists he took with him stemmed the beginnings of Egyptology. The French continued to regard the whole northern coast of Africa, including Egypt, as their legitimate sphere, and it was not until the construction of the Suez canal that the British took an interest. In 1875 the British government bought a major shareholding in the Suez Canal. Egypt was then nominally a part of the Turkish Empire but, in practice, its dynasty of khedives, who came from Albania, were independent rulers.

Although in many ways cultured and elegant, the Egyptian upper classes, including the ruling dynasty, tended towards corruption and greed. They accepted European loans and investment, but sometimes dissipated the money, paying interest out of capital. This was not entirely against British interests because it was due to his indebtedness that the Khedive Ismail was forced to sell out his share in the Suez Canal to the British at knock-down price. However, in 1876 the Egyptian administration became totally bankrupt and Ismail was induced to have British and French commissioners controlling his affairs. The policy of the London government was at this time against the annexation of Egypt—it wanted merely to try to salvage investments.

The appearance of alien officials at the heart of their government antagonised many Egyptians and, in a nationalist revolt, Colonel Arabi of the Egyptian army seized power and set about expelling foreigners and persecuting Christians. Rioting pro-Arabi crowds committed murders in the streets. After much hestitation, the Liberal government of W. E. Gladstone ordered the bombardment of Alexandria and then landed an army under Lord Wolseley which defeated Arabi's forces at the battle of Tel-el-Kebir in September 1882. (The French, for largely domestic reasons of their own, had declined to join the expedition.) From this moment Egypt became, in effect, a British colony with the British agent and consul general the *de facto* supreme authority. Gladstone had not expected this—he had intended the occupation to be only temporary.

However it turned out to be easier to become enmeshed in Egypt than to get out again. The British agent, Evelyn Baring (later earl of Cromer) was a member of a London banking family, and he decided that Egyptian finances would take years

to get straight. Since Gladstone, too, was a believer in the more puritanical methods of money management, with investments being safe and dividends paid regularly, he fell in with this. (The canal and the route to India were also a constant factor in the background.) Through more or less accidental circumstances British imperial and patriotic pride also became involved.

In the Sudan, over which Egypt claimed suzerainty (it had been a useful area for capturing slaves), there arose a visionary Moslem religious leader, the Mahdi, who whipped up the people into a form of nationalist revolt against the Egyptian administration. A British-led expedition of the Egyptian army was annihilated by the Mahdi's men. The Gladstone cabinet, who, whether they liked it or not, were now running Egypt, decided to let the Mahdi have the Sudan and appointed General Charles Gordon to organise the evacuation of the Egyptian army garrisons.

General Gordon

Gordon was an army engineer and a minor public hero who had served variously in China, India, the Crimea, Ireland, Mauritius, Sudan and the Cape. He was noted for extreme physical courage and may have been slightly mad. He believed in the Bible not only in the sense that he thought every word was literally true but also in the sense that it contained prophecies hidden in secret codes. He governed his actions by his own, highly personalised interpretations of biblical prophecies. He went to Palestine and, using his engineer's training, conducted a detailed survey of the Christian holy places; he collated masses of measurements against the biblical stories and tried to use them to foretell the future. He was a solitary alcoholic, sometimes retiring for days on end with his Bible and his bottles. He was also a bachelor. To the general public he tended to be extolled as a great Christian soldier.

Once he was in the Sudan, Gordon disobeyed his orders and decided to try to hold the territory against his fellow religious fanatic, the Mahdi. Whether he did this for mystical reasons or on the basis of a rational judgment can only be guessed at, but at any rate he shut himself up in the capital of Khartoum and refused to budge. As communications with him were cut off by the advancing Mahdi, the British newspapers and public began to get almost as excited as though Gordon had been a second Livingstone. He became a political issue in London, the Conservative opposition claiming that he had been abandoned. After some delay, the Gladstone administration sent an expedition to rescue him, but it arrived at Khartoum to find that two days earlier the Mahdi's troops had occupied the city and killed him. Queen Victoria, in one of her rare interventions in imperial matters, was so incensed that she sent Gladstone an uncoded telegram over the public wire blaming him for Gordon's death.

Kitchener of Khartoum

The Conservatives made much political capital out of the Gordon episode and, on their return to power, the professedly imperialist Joseph Chamberlain, the colonial secretary, took the lead in plans to reconquer the Sudan. The motives were partly revenge for Gordon, and partly a legitimate fear that the French would penetrate the territory from the west and thus command the Egyptian hinterland. Equipped with newly-issued machine guns, an Anglo-Egyptian army set off from Egypt under the command of another bachelor army engineer, Horatio Herbert Kitchener, and he routed the Mahdi at the battle of Omdurman in 1898. This battle saw the last formal cavalry charge in the history of the British Army – one of the officers who took part in it was the young Winston Churchill of the fourth Hussars. The Mahdi was killed in the battle and Kitchener had his skull made into an ink pot. On being created a peer, he proudly took the title 'Kitchener of Khartoum' and for the rest of his life he was a major public personality, with much political influence.

Egypt and the Sudan always had a special position within the imperial system. They were governed through the Foreign Office instead of through the Colonial Office. The Sudan

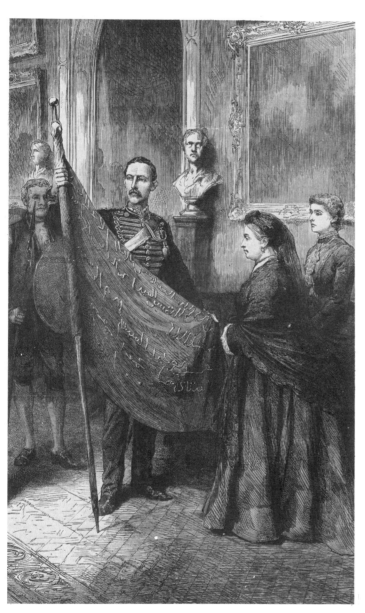

The Battle of Omdurman, at which the Mahdi was finally routed by an Anglo-Egyptian army under the command of Kitchener. The Mahdi was killed in the battle and Kitchener had his skull made into an inkpot.

A trophy from the Sudan – Lieutenant Wilford Lloyd presents one of the Mahdi's flags to the queen.

The Mahdi, the visionary Moslem religious leader in the Sudan, who whipped up his people to a revolt against the Egyptian administration, and wiped out a British-led expedition of the Egyptian army.

became, officially, an Anglo-Egyptian 'condominium', although in practice it was entirely British-directed. Evelyn Baring was an efficient administrator and built up a civil service of expatriates, but the Egyptians never really accepted their subordinate status. Relationships between the British and the Egyptians were the worst in the empire. In the Sudan the British were more successful: a club-like little Sudan civil service, consisting of men who spent their whole working lives in the territory, built up a genuine fund of goodwill, especially among the non-Arab inhabitants. To many Sudanese, the British appeared to be a lesser evil than their Egyptian predecessors.

The Pacific Islands

The religious impulse in the British people at home which had sustained Livingstone and Gordon had its deepest social results in the islands of the Pacific Ocean. Early missionaries, many of them Calvinist, meant well but had no appreciation of the destruction they caused. The characteristic South Sea islanders were cheerful peoples who devoted much of their time to ceremonial dancing and singing and to uninhibited sexual relationships. Some of them also practised a ritualistic form of cannibalism. They were brilliant seamen. The Victorian missionaries, supported by British power, suppressed 'immoral' customs. There was some resistance – a British missionary in Fiji was killed, boiled and eaten as late as 1867 – but on the whole the people were cowed. Forced to wash and wear clothes, they caught European deseases and died. In a single year, 1875, a quarter of the population of Fiji died from measles, a disease brought by the Europeans to which they had no natural immunity.

In addition to the missionaries came traders and prospectors, some of whom were no better than raiders. The islands were ravaged with syphillis and many of the male population were 'blackbirded' to work virtually as slaves in the sugar plantations of Queensland. The missionaries, who became better informed as time went on, pressed for British colonial administration as the only hope of producing order. This came, step by step, in the latter part of the nineteenth century, the islands being shared out among the British, the French and the Germans. The Philippines, which had long been Spanish, went to the United States.

The West Indies

The slums of the Victorian empire were its oldest section, the West Indies. The abolition of slavery followed by free trade, which robbed their sugar of preferential treatment in the British market, broke their economy, and relatively little was done to assist them. It seemed that British energies were too fully absorbed in other parts of the world to pay much attention to the West Indies. Anthony Trollope, who visited Jamaica in 1858, wrote: 'Her roads are almost impassable, her bridges are broken down, her coffee plantations have gone back to bush, her sugar estates have been sold for the value of the sugar boilers. Kingston as a town is the most deplorable that man has ever visited, unless it be that Spanish Town is worse.' Compared with, for example, Spanish Cuba in the same part of the world, the British West Indies were a disgrace. Yet the inhabitants, mostly former slaves and their descendants, remained cheerfully pro-British. Only one episode brought them vividly before British public opinion and that was one of savage suppression.

Partly from Baptist revivalism and partly from economic hardship, a relatively small riot broke out in Morant Bay, Jamaica, in 1865. A trigger-happy local militia began shooting and it turned into serious disorder with crowds burning public buildings and killing between fifteen and twenty white men.

The governor, Edward Eyre, appeared to lose his nerve and embarked upon wholesale reprisals. Hitherto his record had been quite a good one. He had served with distinction in Australia and there had been nothing to suggest that he was a sadist. However there was a definite strain of sadism in one or two of his officials and they were allowed full freedom to exercise it.

In the immediate aftermath of the riots, eighty-five people were shot or hanged without trial. Then a further 354 were executed after trial by court martial. There were thousands of floggings of both men and women. It was enough to be a known Baptist preacher to be ordered summarily to receive fifty lashes. One man was hanged because, mid-way through a flogging, he turned and ground his teeth at the officer in charge. When reports of the incident reached London, Eyre was recalled and a special investigating commission was sent out to Jamaica, which reported that Eyre had behaved with 'skill, promptitude and vigour' in suppressing a revolt but had allowed excessive and 'positively barbarous' punishments.

Liberalism and imperialism

Eyre's conduct became a big political issue in London, a 'Jamaica Committee' being formed of such liberals as John Stuart Mill, Herbert Spencer, T. H. Huxley and Thomas Hughes to prosecute him for murder. Funds to support the prosecution came from missionary societies. Eyre's sympathisers, who included Thomas Carlyle, John Ruskin, Alfred Lord Tennyson and Charles Kingsley, formed a 'Governor Eyre Defence Committee' to pay for his defence. For five years in the newspapers, the House of Commons and the law courts, many of the giants of Victorian England raged against each other over what Eyre had done. Eyre's opponents failed to overcome preliminary legal technicalities in their murder prosecution but the very fact that such a controversy was waged on such a scale is a significant pointer to the nature of British Empire in the nineteenth century. The British Victorians were not a monolithic force but were divided and argumentative, operating from a range of widely different motives.

In the early and middle period of Victoria's reign there had been considerable controversy in London about whether it was really worthwhile extending the British Empire. Such Liberal free traders as Richard Cobden and John Bright argued actively against the acquisition of new colonies. 'Our dependencies,' wrote Cobden, 'serve but as gorgeous and ponderous appendages, without improving our balance of trade'. Even the young Disraeli, who later became a romantic imperialist, wrote in 1852 'these wretched colonies will all be independent, and are a millstone around our necks'. By the end of Victoria's reign, however, such views had gone out of fashion. The Conservative Party was definitely imperialist and such Liberal leaders as Asquith, Rosebery and Charles Dilke had also adopted an imperialist position. The more radical Liberals, such as John Morley, Henry Campbell-Bannerman and the young David Lloyd George, opposed what they regarded as oppression and cruelty but took the actual existence of the empire for granted.

By far the best-known politician in the public eye in the 1890s was Joseph Chamberlain of Birmingham. Although he never became prime minister, Chamberlain typified much of his times. A largely self-made industrial tycoon (he manufactured screws), he had entered politics as a radical and, indeed, a republican. As mayor of Birmingham, he cleaned up and beautified his native city. He came into national politics as a definitely regional force, more on an American than a British pattern, basing himself upon the Birmingham Liberal Party machine, which marshalled the newly-enfranchised mass electorate. Slim, tall, commanding, an orchid in his buttonhole and monocle at his eye, Chamberlain was powerful as an orator both on the public platform and in the House of Commons. He believed imperialism was good for business and thus for the prosperity of Birmingham.

When W. E. Gladstone, as Liberal prime minister, attempted to introduce home rule for Ireland, Chamberlain broke away from him on the ground that to break the unity of the United Kingdom would be to wound the empire at its very heart. Thereafter his Liberal Unionists worked closely with the Conservatives; Birmingham went with him. In 1895 Chamberlain, who was powerful enough to choose what post he wanted in a new Conservative government, decided to become colonial secretary. This caused some surprise for that office had not been

regarded as one of the top rank. He used the post to work vigorously for the expansion and consolidation of the British Empire; he was the first colonial secretary really to do this. One result was the Boer War, which was still raging when Queen Victoria died in 1901. It was the first hint that the twentieth century might not be so triumphant for the British as the nineteenth had been.

Fijian warriors. The Pacific islands were among the casualties of the Victorian missionary impulse: well-meaning, but with little idea of the havoc they were causing, the missionaries suppressed 'immoral' customs, and forced the inhabitants to wash and to wear clothes, whereupon many of them caught European diseases and died.

The union jack is hoisted at Port Moresby, New Guinea in 1884, when the British proclaimed a protectorate over the south-east coast and adjacent islands.

*The sugar mill at Montego Bay,
Jamaica. The West Indies were
the slums of the Victorian empire:
the abolition of slavery, and then
free trade, had caused a serious
decline in the sugar industry, and
by the middle of the nineteenth
century overpopulation and poverty
were giving rise to frequent riots.*

Edward John Eyre, governor of
Jamaica, whose vicious punitive
measures after a riot in 1865
became a major political issue in
London, where the climate of
opinion was becoming progressively
more humanitarian.

Joseph Chamberlain with his wife.
Chamberlain served under
Gladstone as Liberal president of
the Board of Trade, but resigned
over Home Rule for Ireland. As
leader of the Liberal-Unionists,
and then as colonial secretary in
the new Conservative government,
he worked vigorously for the
expansion and consolidation of the
empire.

The sun never sets

Lord Curzon, Viceroy of India from 1899 to 1905, was one of the highest paid men in public service at the time; he had absolute power over 300 million Indians, not to mention the vast bureaucracy of British officialdom, whose most senior members he treated as though they were little more than clerks. An arrogant, though incredibly hard-working man, he behaved almost as an independent monarch - he at one time considered annexing Persia - aiming to fasten British rule even more closely on India.

The British Empire died young. It began to reach maturity in the early twentieth century, and by the middle of the same century was in active and rapid dissolution. In some imperial territories it was possible for a man in his lifetime to see the span of the whole British colonial period. Thus, for example, Jomo Kenyatta was a child when the British took over his country, Kenya, but he lived to take over the British power himself.

Lord Curzon

If any single person epitomised the British Empire at its most powerful and most apparently stable it was George Nathaniel Curzon, Viceroy of India from 1899 to 1905. He was an able, arrogant hard-working man who took if for granted that, though he was only thirty-eight, he should assume absolute power over 300 million Indians, one sixth of the human race, as a sort of detour on the way to the British prime ministership, which he also expected to achieve. With his rich American wife beside him, he lived in a quasi-royal state, riding on ceremonial elephants and expecting women to curtsey to him. Behind the scenes he worked far into the night in a superhuman effort to keep account of every aspect of administration.

The Indian Middle-class political party, the National Congress, which was working for the growth of Indian self-government, gave Curzon a respectful address of welcome upon his arrival. One of its leaders at that time, G. K. Gokhale, wrote that the British had come to India by 'the inscrutable wisdom of Providence'. The future leader of independent India, Jawaharlal Nehru, was at the time at Harrow School, London, and his father, Motilal Nehru, was a successful lawyer who wore western dress and regarded himself as fully integrated into the British system. Mohandas Karamchand Gandhi was a lawyer in South Africa and an explicit supporter of the British Empire.

Curzon, who had previously been Under-Secretary of State for Foreign Affairs in a Conservative government, landed at Bombay on 30 December, 1898, to a salute of thirty-one guns. His ceremonial cavalry bodyguard, in scarlet tunics, escorted him to the railway station where he took the special, white vice-regal train to Calcutta, his capital. In his first month he entertained 3,500 guests to meals, all eaten off silver plate. Although his salary of £16,720 a year (equivalent to about £100,000 a year tax-free in 1970) was the highest in the British public service – three times that of the prime minister – Curzon found it too small to live on in what he regarded as a suitable manner. He supplemented it with £16,000 a year from his father-in-law, a self-made Chicago meat millionaire, and the meagre £1,000 a year which was all his own aristocratic but relatively poor family could allow him.

In the half century since the mutiny, official British India had become a fully-functioning organism with its own momentum. The 'India Office List' for the year of Curzon's appointment set out in small type in 700 pages the title, biography, duties and salary of every British official in India, from bishops to railway engineers. The elite Indian Civil Service, of 1,200 members, was supplemented by a million locally-recruited clerks. It was a pompous society with a strong sense of self-importance and hierarchy. The administration was slow but efficient, with masses of paperwork written out by pen and ink under fans worked manually by 'punkah-Wallahs'. In town the characteristic method of transport for a British official was by rickshaw, drawn by one or two coolies; in Simla, because of the hilly terrain, sometimes four coolies drew one sahib. For a longer distance an official would travel by train on a journey that might take him several days to cross India. The railways, which ran at a sound profit, were one of the major achievements of the British Indian administration.

Curzon mastered this vast bureaucracy and treated even the most senior officials in it, men with knighthoods, as if they were clerks. His aim was to speed it up and modernise it and, indeed, the electric shock he gave it was of lasting value, up to and beyond independence less than half a century later. Curzon, however, had not the least presentiment that he was preparing India for relatively early independence. Like other Englishmen of his class he had been educated in the classics and thus knew much about the Roman Empire which had lasted five centuries in full flower. While, doubtless, the British Empire would not last for ever, it must be at least as glorious as that of Rome. At a magnificent *durbar* (reception) to mark the coronation of Edward VII – it was far more elaborate than the ceremonies in London – Curzon banned the singing of *Onward Christian Soldiers* because it contained the words, 'thrones and crowns may perish, kingdoms rise and fall'.

In foreign affairs, Curzon behaved almost as an independent monarch. His aim was to strengthen India's defences at the north-west frontier, where Russia was regarded as a menace, and in the Persian Gulf, where there was fear of German penetration, Curzon considered annexing Persia, and sent an expedition to conquer the Chinese subordinate territory of Tibet. Curzon's forces had no difficulty in defeating the army of the god-king of Tibet, the Dalai Lama, but London in the end vetoed annexation.

In domestic Indian affairs, Curzon's aim was to fasten British rule on India more closely than ever before. He behaved autocratically towards the princes and hoped to hasten the demise of the Indian National Congress. He abolished the city council of Calcutta which had an elected Indian majority. He tried to overhaul the universities so they would have fewer students but of higher quality. He partitioned Bengal into two provinces on grounds of administrative efficiency. The net result of all this, however, was to speed up the growth of middle-class nationalism, which threw up a small violent wing under the leadership of the newspaper editor B. G. Tilak. In particular the partition of Bengal, India's biggest and most advanced province, aroused intellectual resentment. By the end of his reign Curzon was having to employ censorship and police repression to hold down hostile public opinion.

His departure, however, had nothing to do with Indian opinion. It arose from one of the most monumental personal rivalries in the history of the British Empire. Curzon asked that Lord Kitchener, the hero of Khartoum and of the Boer War, be made commander-in-chief in India. One motive, probably, was vanity – Curzon wanted to have the most famous soldier in the empire under his jurisdiction. However, Kitchener was himself a commanding personality, who had influence among British politicians as well as high standing in British public opinion. He had not the slightest intention of being treated as a subordinate, and resisted the attempts of the viceroy to control the army as closely as he controlled everything else in India. Curzon decided to use the ultimate weapon of threatening to resign if London would not support him against Kitchener. To his surprise and humiliation, the prime minister, A. J. Balfour, accepted his resignation and Curzon had to quit his palaces and sail home.

Military power

If Curzon represented the patrician stream in early twentieth-century Britain – he took it for granted that he had been born to rule not only the subject peoples of the empire but also the British lower classes – Kitchener represented sheer military power. On the whole, straight-forward military conquest had not been the principal means of extending the empire but, so far as it existed, Kitchener epitomised it. Kitchener was a mysterious character whom nobody ever knew well. There was an hypnotic quality to him – a picture of his face was the most

A painting by Tom Roberts showing the Duke of York (later King George V) opening Australia's first Federal Parliament in the Exhibition building at Melbourne in 1901.

Left: the Delhi Durbar of 1903, in which Lord and Lady Curzon marked the accession of Edward VII.

successful army recruiting poster ever devised – and he carried himself with enormous natural authority. He was not outstandingly clever, and his skill as a general lay in his ability to carry out commonsense decisions.

Kitchener had made his first reputation with the capture of Khartoum. Then in South Africa he retrieved the British position after their initial defeats at the hands of the Boers. To wipe out guerrilla warfare in the Boer republics, he invented what he called the 'concentration camp'. This entailed the systematic clearing of Boer territory, with the population removed from their homes and confined to prison camps, so that the guerrilla forces lost their bases. Many died in the camps, mainly through typhoid epidemics, and the British fell into some international discredit. However, Kitchener was not being sadistic and certainly was not thinking in terms of genocide; in his stolid way he was merely clearing up a mess by what seemed to be the only available military methods. In the House of Commons in London, the leader of the Liberal opposition, Sir Henry Campbell-Bannerman, called them 'methods of barbarism', a phrase which infuriated the government, but the fact that it could be used by the shadow prime minister was an indication of the contrary streams which existed in British politics even at the height of the imperial period.

The new Liberal government

In 1905 Campbell-Bannerman became prime minister at the head of an unusually brilliant Liberal government which won a landslide majority in the House of Commons. While the

election had been won on mainly domestic issues it did, in a real sense, represent a British reaction against extreme imperialism. Joseph Chamberlain. with his dream of strengthening and extending the British Empire, had proposed an imperial customs union with tariffs on non-imperial imports and a measure of free trade within the empire itself. Had this ever become a reality, the empire might well have grown into an organic economic unit which would have been difficult ever to dismantle. In practice, however, neither the self-governing dominions nor the British public wanted it. The dominions wanted to run their own economics and build up their own industries. The British public was not prepared to pay the higher food prices a protectionist policy would have entailed.

The new Liberal ministers found themselves ruling something approaching a third of the human race. While they had no idea of dismantling the empire and, indeed, lacked any coherent long-term policy for it, they did inject a measure of classical British radicalism into it. Curzon had left India seething with middle-class nationalist agitation, and the remedy of the Liberal secretary of state for India, the philosopher-politician John Morley, was to take the first, cautious steps towards self-government. In retrospect they seem mild enough – the introduction of an elected element to the legislatures on a limited franchise and the appointment of an Indian to the viceroy's cabinet – but at the time they were furiously attacked in Britain by Curzon and other Conservatives as presaging the break-up of the British Indian Empire. In a sense, of course, Curzon was correct.

In South Africa the Liberal ministers allowed self-government to the defeated Boer republics and went on to unite them with the British provinces of Cape Colony and Natal into the Union of South Africa; it was characteristic of the times, however, that almost no account was taken of black South Africans who formed the majority of the population. The phrase 'racial

The railways, which ran at a sound profit, were among the lasting benefits of British rule as well as being major engineering achievements. Above: the Darjeeling-Himalayan railway; the loop at Chambatta. Top right: the Kalka-Simla railway.

New Delhi. Above: *general secretarial building. In the early years
of the twentieth century the capital was removed from the coastal town
of Calcutta to Delhi, and the architect Edwin Lutyens was
commissioned to design New Delhi as the British capital, complete
with viceregal palace, offices for the bureaucracy and a parliament
building for the central legislature.*

strife' in South Africa in the first decade of the twentieth century referred to disputes between British and Boers; anything connected with Africans was 'the native problem'. For a while the policy of British friendship towards the Boers really worked and a group of Boer leaders arose, the most notable of whom was Jan Christian Smuts, who were sincerely faithful to the British connection. In the long run it proved to be a failure but, in the meantime, it had given the British a false idea of the capacity of their institutions to encompass non-British peoples.

Kenya

It was largely under Liberal administration that an entirely new white colony suddenly flowered in Kenya. It sprang partly from the rakish and adventurous Lord Delamere, a young peer who loved roaming around Africa on private expeditions. He entered Kenya from Somalia and chanced upon the cool highlands which seemed to be another Britain, except that they were more beautiful. They also seemed to be empty since the indigenous inhabitants, the Kikuyu, had come near to being wiped out by typhoid. Delamere settled in the highlands and began to farm them.

At the same time the Uganda railway, which ran from the coast to the Uganda protectorate, was completed. The original purpose of the railway – a brilliant engineering achievement – had been to underpin the British administration of Uganda, which had been acquired on the pretext of protecting the source of the Nile, and thus Egypt and the route to India. Until the railway was built, British officials in Uganda were allowed six months on top of their normal leaves because they had had to walk the 800 miles to the coast. The railway had to cross Kenya which, therefore, had to be incorporated within the empire. The problem was to make the railway pay for itself, since the Uganda traffic was not sufficient for it. The obvious answer was to encourage white settlement in the highlands, which were coolly proclaimed to be 'crown' territory, with the Kikuyu put into 'reservations'. Encouraged by Delamere's example and leadership, adventurous British colonisers rattled up the new railway, acquired long leases of 'crown' land at exceptionally low prices and, with many incidental difficulties, began to build a prosperous agriculture. To make the Africans work on the new farms, a 'hut tax' was imposed which had to be paid in cash.

By 1914 there were 6,000 Europeans in Kenya and they were already clamouring for self-government on the South African model. However, in the last resort, the British always maintained that Kenya was an African as well as a white colony; although the settlers were allowed an elected legislature, final power remained with the governor appointed by the Colonial Office in London. Actually the white immigrants were greatly outnumbered by the Indians, who had come originally as labour to build the railway and stayed on to become the mainstay of the economy of a new urban Kenya in Nairobi and Mombasa. The term 'white highlands' was not really directed against the Africans but against the Indian immigrants, who were not allowed to farm within them. By the 1920s it had become a temporary demand of Indian nationalists, both in Kenya and in India, for Kenya to be removed from Colonial Office control and put under the Government of India.

The 'Mad Mullah'

Meanwhile, in the neighbouring territory of British Somaliland, a religious-nationalist leader, Mahomed bin Abdillah Hassab, was conducting a prolonged rebellion against British rule. This was an arid, sparsely populated territory with tribes which migrated around it in search of water and for twenty years Hassab kept his forces free from British authority. He wrote to the British commander: 'I like war but you do not. The country is a jungle and that is no use to you. If you want wood and stone you can get them in plenty. There are also many ant-heaps. The sun is very hot.'

The British, who had acquired the place only for the purpose of protecting the route to India, cheerfully nicknamed Hassab 'the Mad Mullah' (a term indicative of British attitudes of the period), and sent occasional expeditions to try to suppress him. However, their authority was really secure only on the coast and it was not until 1920, with the use of the new weapon of air power, that the 'Mad Mullah', who shortly afterwards died of influenza, was defeated.

The King Emperor

With the accession of King George V in 1910, the British Empire at last acquired a monarch who was deeply and continuously interested in it. George had served as a regular naval officer and seen much of it for himself. In particular he took his strange title of 'Emperor of India' with great seriousness. Despite the hesitations of his Liberal ministers he insisted on sailing out to India to inaugurate his reign in person. He was the only reigning British monarch ever to have visited India and he surrounded himself with splendour. At the old Moghul capital of Delhi he reviewed an enormous parade of troops and, crowned and seated under a canopy in the open air, received the homage of the Indian princes. However, the crown, although specially

Lord Kitchener, hero of Khartoum and the Boer War, was sent to India as commander-in-chief of British forces at the request of Lord Curzon. However, he refused to allow the army to be closely controlled, as was everything else in India, by the viceroy, and friction developed between them which resulted in Curzon, in a last attempt to gain support from London, threatening resignation. To his surprise his resignation was accepted.

Left: Jan Christian Smuts who, although he had renounced his British citizenship and commanded guerilla forces during the Boer War, later became convinced that the British connection was essential to the greatness of South Africa.

made for India, was taken back to London lest it fall into the hands of Indian insurrectionists.

To stress the permanence of British rule in India, the capital at this time was removed from the British-founded coastal settlement of Calcutta to ancient Delhi in the middle of the sub-continent. Most British officials disliked the change, but the motivation behind it was to make the administration seem more integral to India and less an alien thing based upon a port. The architect Edwin Lutyens was commissioned to design New Delhi, next to the Moghul city, as the custom-built British capital, complete with viceregal palace, splendid offices for the bureaucracy and a parliament building for the central legislature. By the time this was finished, however, the British were already negotiating with Gandhi and the Nehrus the first stages in what proved to be the rapid abandonment of power.

George V also took seriously his duties as head of state of the self-governing territories of Canada, Newfoundland, Australia, New Zealand and South Africa. In 1907 their designation had been officially changed from 'colony' to 'dominion' and the occasional London meetings of their prime ministers were termed the 'Imperial Conference' instead of the 'Colonial Conference'; until the First World War, however, it was the British colonial secretary, not the prime minister, who presided. The king actively tried to insist that the posts of governors-general of the dominions should be held by men personally congenial to him. He was also clear-headed enough to see that organic unity could only be maintained if the London government were allowed a degree of precedence over the others. He tried, unsuccessfully, to insist that formal 'advice' to him should come only from the British prime minister, thus removing the possibility that he might receive conflicting 'advice' from different sets of ministers, with the crown and the empire thus reduced to meaningless formalities.

The First World War

As always, even when the world-wide British Empire was apparently a crucial factor in British policy, the British in the last resort were Europeans. They entered the Frist World War, their greatest conflict ever, for reasons connected, ultimately, with a dispute in the Balkans and more immediately, because they wanted to prevent the vigorous power of Imperial Germany becoming the leading force on the European continent. As always, the British preferred a divided Europe with no power predominant. They entered this essentially European conflict with the highest enthusiasm, young men 'voting with their feet' by voluntarily joining the army in their hundreds of thousands.

For the first time ever, Britain became a major military power on the mainland of Europe, and what effect this would have on the world-wide empire was a secondary consideration. Government and public alike were fascinated by 'gallant little Belgium', which had resisted an attempt by Germany to attack France across its territory. However, colonial rivalries were part of the total background and there was an element in Germany which felt jealous of the fact that the British had acquired so much territory. The Germans had antagonised the British by building a battle fleet which seemed to imperil the British mastery of the seas on which the empire appeared to depend. With much vociferous support from public opinion on both sides, Britian and Germany had been engaging in a naval arms race.

In the east, Germany defeated Russia, which soon after turned Communist. In the west there was a prolonged and bloody stalemate, broken by the prospect of the United States intervening in the war on a massive scale. Germany, in conditions of internal chaos, was forced to sign a punitive peace treaty which, among other things, stripped her of her colonies. As in the 1815 Congress of Vienna, the bulk of the enemy colonies went to Britain, although this time they were to 'mandate' under the supervision of the League of Nations rather than become Britain's absolute property. The local populations were not consulted.

Superficially, therefore, the First World War seemed to represent a vast strengthening of the British Empire. This seemed to happen at two levels; political and territorial.

Politically, the self-governing dominions appeared to move towards a closer union with Britian. They had no choice about being involved in the war for, by law, they were bound by the British declaration. However, Britain could not actually force them to provide troops, and the fact that they did so on a considerable scale and with enthusiasm was evidence that the 'mother country' commanded much emotional loyalty. French Quebec held somewhat aloof from the prevailing Canadian enthusiasm and there was an anti-war rising in South Africa, put down by local South African troops, but on the whole the dominions supported the war on a scale that surprised the Germans (the British ought to have been surprised but, in practice, took it all for granted). Of course there were some local issues involved – both South Africa and Australia were interested in acquiring German colonies adjacent to them – but the major force was sheer imperial patriotism. Smuts, who had fought the British in the Boer War, now put on a British uniform to lead a campaign against the Germans. Later he went to London and served as a full member of the British War Cabinet.

The war spawned new political devices. Dominion prime ministers visited London and their meetings were termed the 'Imperial War Cabinet', which was supposed to be the supreme directing force in the British conduct of the war. Actually, despite such terminology, it was as much an international negotiation as a 'cabinet' in the ordinary sense of the term.

The war was really directed partly by the lively, radical prime minister, David Lloyd George, and partly by the British generals in the field, who, due to their influence with the king, had a wide measure of independent authority (Lloyd George, being leader of no party, lacked the full authority of his office). However, there was such an air of imperial unity that constitution-mongers busied themselves with schemes to turn the self-governing sections of the empire into a federation, with a central government to run foreign policy and defence. Such schemes had been drifting around for twenty years or more – Joseph Chamberlain had been interested in them – but they broke down on the central point that in terms of population Britain was over twice the size of all the self-governing dominions put together. On any principle of equal representation, therefore, she would dominate the structure and thus the dominions would lose control of their own affairs. And the British would certainly have not agreed to their vital interests being swamped in a body analogous to the United States senate in which each member of the federation had an equal vote. The informal method of consultation between prime ministers was the only means of unity – the British prime minister now played a full part, the colonial secretary, so far as the dominions were concerned, having become only a channel of communication.

In 1919 the Imperial Conference piously resolved that in future it would meet more frequently than in pre-war days and that the members would closely co-ordinate their policies. This turned out to be so much hot air. Within a couple of years the British were threatening to declare war on Turkey with no previous dominion consultation and the intervals between imperial conferences steadily lengthened.

The real political result of the war for the dominions was to make them more, not less, independent. Except for Newfoundland, which ultimately was to federate with Canada, they signed the peace treaty as independent states. South Africa and Australia had former German colonies mandated to them. All except Newfoundland became full members of the League of Nations. By 1923 Canada was making a treaty with the United States on her own authority, with no British signature.

The territorial results sprang partly from the annexation of German colonies and partly from the collapse of the old Turkish Empire, the power which for centuries had controlled the Middle East and which had sided with Germany in the war. Making generous use of Indian troops, paid for by India, and enlisting, on false premises, the support of Arab nationalists, the British conquered Mesopotamia (Iraq), Palestine and Syria from the Turks and occupied Persia (Iran). Egypt, which had long been a British colony for all practical purposes, was formally annexed.

In accordance with a previous agreement to partition the spoils, the British handed Syria over to the French against the vigorous protests of its Arab leaders. Curzon, now foreign secretary, thought of holding on to Persia but was overruled. Mesopotamia and Palestine, however, were mandated to Britain, and such glamorous cities as Bagdad and Jerusalem entered the British Empire. The British found this an exciting process, and a former Oxford don, T. E. Lawrence, who had served as liasion officer with the Arab nationalists, was fêted as 'Lawrence of Arabia'. In fact Lawrence, a gifted thinker who was also a masochist and a compulsive liar, was less significant than the public supposed – he belonged more to the Gordon tradition of imperialists than the Lugard one.

Altogether the First World War added, if Egypt is counted, well over one million square miles of extra territory to the British Empire, an area nine times that of Britain herself, with a popula-

Above: *Australian troops cross a duckboard track through the remains of Château forest, Passchendaele, 1917.*

Right: *British Mark V tanks allotted to the 5th Australian division moving up for the Allied assault on the Hindenburg line.*

Indian recruiting poster. The text reads: 'This soldier is guarding India. He is guarding his home and his household. Thus we are guarding your home. You have to join the army.' Nearly one million Indians did so.

300,000 CANADIANS

HAVE JOINED THE COLORS

AND ARE HELPING TO CRUSH THIS VENOMOUS REPTILE.

Two hundred thousand will yet answer the call that says:

Your King and Country Need You

Will YOU Be One of These?

The Forces of the ALLIES are Exerting Every Ounce of Their Strength to CHAIN this DRAGON.

Will YOU HELP Along With the Other LOYAL SONS of Britain?

JOIN the 99th ESSEX BATTALION and HELP CRUSH the GERMAN MONSTER The World-wide Menace to Humanity and Civilization.

For particulars Apply to

Lieut. Morton

Wellington Barracks or W. T. Gregory at 141 Talbot St.

LAW AND ORDER

GERMAN-AMERICAN TREASON AND TREACHERY

"These have poured the poison of disloyalty into the very arteries of our national life; have sought to bring the authority and good name of our Government into contempt, to destroy our industries wherever they thought it effective for their vindictive purposes to strike at them, and to debase our politics to the uses of foreign intrigue. Such creatures of passion, disloyalty and anarchy must be crushed out."

[By Courtesy Montreal Star.]

—President Wilson.

A Canadian recruiting poster. Conscription, introduced in Canada in 1917, was opposed by many French Canadians, but welcomed by most of English-speaking Canada.

tion totalling about twenty-five million. Britain entered the jazz age of the 1920s with her territories at their greatest extent and her most dangerous European rival, Germany, completely broken.

Middle East problems

But the great new empire in the Middle East represented little but trouble. The Iraqis were so awkward that the British quickly divested themselves of them. The Egyptians then, as always, disliked British rule, but the British felt they had to stay in order to guard the Suez Canal. They quickly set up the originally Albanian dynasty of khedives as kings of Egypt but, in conditions of frequent riot and assassination, insisted on a 'treaty' relationship by which they controlled Egypt's defence and foreign affairs and, in practice, also had the last word in internal matters.

Yet more troublesome was Palestine, over which definitely contradictory promises had been given with results that ought to have been predictable at the time they were made. The Arabs thought that Palestine would become an Arab state, probably joined with Syria. At the most there would have been a period of mandate, as happened in Iraq. But the British had also promised Palestine as 'a national home' for the Jews.

Had there been plenty of time and no persecutions of the Jews in Poland in the 1920s and in Germany in the 1930s and early 1940s, the British might just have managed to contain their contradictory promises. Palestine in 1918 had only half a million Arabs and so there was plenty of room for Jewish Zionist immigrants, who paid for the land they occupied. There had been Jewish inhabitants of Palestine for some 3,000 years and, at least for several centuries, they had had no particular conflict with the Arabs. Anti-semitism had been a European, not an Arab, activity. Militant Zionism, which sought to establish a Jewish state in Palestine, was a European phenomenon and its leaders had a characteristically European attitude of the period of regarding the Arabs as only 'natives'. Chaim Weizmann, the main leader, believed that it was a part of the Jewish mission in Palestine to raise the living standards of the Arabs.

Under pressure of persecution in Europe, Jews arrived in Palestine in larger numbers than could be accommodated peacefully. The Arab population also rose, Arabs migrating to Palestine because of the prosperity the Jews had brought. By the 1930s the two communities were in bitter conflict, with the British incapable of reconciling them. British attempts to limit Jewish immigration at the moment when the dictator of Germany was intent upon the physical extermination of Jews could bring them nothing but international discredit. After the Second World War, the British simply abandoned Palestine and separate Jewish and Arab states were created, leading to a Middle East instability which continued for many years afterwards.

Indian nationalism

In India, also, the British position was becoming more difficult to maintain. The First World War had been fought partly on the premise that the weaker European nationalities should be allowed independence and such states as Poland, Czechoslovakia and Yugoslavia had come into existence free from their former overlords. This example of national self-determination struck the imagination of the Indian middle-classes. At the same time a million Indians, mostly from the Punjab, had served in the wartime army and thus greatly broadened their experience – some had served even on the Western Front in Belgium. The mystical Mohandas Karamchand Gandhi renounced his belief in the British Empire, left South Africa for India and launched a campaign for 'soul force' and 'non-violent' agitation against British rule. Through Gandhi's preaching, Indian nationalism was converted from an intellectual middle-class force into a genuine popular movement. Backing up Gandhi were the Nehrus, father and son. Old Motilal Nehru, the wealthy lawyer of Allahabad, put on native Indian dress and led the opposition to the British in the new central legislature. His son, Jawaharlal darted around the country as the active political organiser of the National Congress.

The British, by past standards, were becoming quite liberal in India. In 1917, to mark appreciation of Indian services in the war, they had for the first time announced that self-government was their ultimate aim in India, and they went on to establish 'dyarchy' in the provinces, with Indian ministers in charge of departments connected with social welfare, and a central legislature elected on a limited franchise. Any hope, however, of British reforms keeping pace with nationalist demands was shattered by the Arritsar massacre of 1919 in which 379 members of a disorderly crowd were shot down in cold blood on the orders of an inefficient British general. After that even the more moderate nationalists had no time for talk of a British 'civilising mission'.

The aim of Gandhi and the Nehrus was to found a united, independent India, but in this they were frustrated by the growth of a separate Moslem Indian agitation under another lawyer, Mahomet Ali Jinnah, and this won majority support in the Moslem community. By the end of the 1930s. British rule in India had worn paper-thin, with Jawaharlal Nehru running his own shadow government based upon congress control of six of India's eight provinces.

The jazz-age empire seemed stable only in Africa and the Far East, where there was a steady process of consolidation and digestion. There were no more Lugards or Rhodeses to roam the continent to pick up new colonies but there grew up a new profession of colonial civil servants. Most of them were drawn from the British public schools, and they were not so intellectual as the Indian Civil Service. They were expected to have gifts of leadership, a calm judicial attitude and complete integrity. On the whole, these objectives were realised, and the expanding British colonial administration in Africa was well staffed. The members expected no financial reward beyond salary and pension but, as in India, were proud to receive honours and decorations. Equipped with collapsible flag-poles and lines of porters, British officials penetrated the most remote jungles to 'advise' African chiefs and dispense justice.

The system was admirably equipped for dealing with 'inferior' peoples, but was irrelevant to a new African middle class which, even between the wars, was beginning to arise in the Gold Coast and Nigeria. In the Far East, too, the British underpinned their power, the main project being the fortification of Singapore as a stronghold against the new power of Japan.

The rise of Adolf Hitler and a militant new Germany in the 1930s made the British again obsessed with Europe. Hitler at any time would have been happy to do a deal by which the British would have supported him in Europe and he would have supported them in the empire, but only a handful of extremists on the British far right ever thought of this as being a realistic possibility. Although Hitler's Germany did have some genuine grievances, the prevailing British view was that it was based upon false principles and that Nazism could not be accepted as the price for saving the British Empire. On 3 September, 1939, Great Britain declared war on Germany in a dispute connected with Poland. The self-governing dominions, who since the Statute of Westminster in 1931 had become completely independent legally, voluntarily followed suit. India, to the fury of the nationalists, was committed to the war without any consultation with her politicians or people.

Left: *the enthusiasm of the British public for the exploits of 'Lawrence of Arabia', who served as liaison officer with the Arab nationalists, and led their revolt against Turkish domination, was part of the general excitement felt at Britain's annexation of parts of the Middle East, which brought such glamorous cities as Baghdad and Jerusalem into the empire.*

Above: *Mohandas Karamchand Gandhi, whose organisation of non-violent agitation against British rule was more than anything else responsible for India gaining independence. Through his preaching Indian nationalism was converted from an intellectual middle-class force into a genuine mass movement.*

Recessional

*Jawaharlal Nehru, first
prime minister of India, who had
fought for his country's freedom
since the Amritsar massacre
of 1919.*

Although as late as the 1930s, and even into the 1940s, many British politicians still spoke of the empire as if it were a permanent thing, it was effectively finished by the Second World War.

To some extent this was due to direct military conquest by the Japanese, who overran Malaya, Singapore and Burma, were at one point poised to invade India and were a grave threat to Australia and New Zealand. While the Japanese militarist dream that swift aggressive action by a well-trained, well-equipped army could form a permanent 'Co-Prosperity Sphere' in the Far East was even more ephemeral than the British imperial dream, it did have enough success to weaken permanently the magical 'prestige' on which the British had relied so much. In particular, the fall of Singapore was a supreme catastrophe. The prime minister of the time, Winston Churchill, described it as 'the greatest disaster to British arms which our history records'. For twenty years the British had been building up Singapore as a naval and military base. The aim had been to make it the impregnable bastion of British power for the whole Far East. Yet on 15 February, 1942, it capitulated, with a garrison of 100,000 men. The causes were bad planning and a failure, up to the last moment, to appreciate Japanese military efficiency.

In the First World War, the empire had been an asset to the British in that it had provided a reservoir of manpower and raw materials and needed very little defending. In the Second World War, in contrast, the empire was under direct attack, and so became a liability. Quite apart from the Japanese, there were Italian-German offensives in the Mediterranean and the Middle East. At one point the Germans, by an attempted *coup d'etat*, almost got control of Iraq, then a satellite of the British Empire. In two years of intense fighting in the desert of North Africa, the Germans and Italians at times came near to conquering the British satellite of Egypt, and with it the Suez Canal. The Italian dictator, Benito Mussolini, was so confident that he even purchased a white horse, on which he intended to ride in triumph into Cairo. Although the British did hold on to Egypt–the decisive moment was the battle of El Alamein in 1942–the campaign had represented a substantial diversion of forces.

More important, however, than actual military campaigns were the political and moral effects of the war. They actively speeded up the process of disintegration.

Wind of change

In the case of the self-governing dominions, the war increased their sense of independence. They rose and trained their own independent defence forces. They exerted independent voices in the new United Nations Organisation. Most significantly of all, they had to cease to look to Britain as their principle military defender. They either had to defend themselves or to look for what allies were most able to assist them, and this meant, in particular, the United States.

Then there was the moral point that Britain had declared war upon Germany in the name of democracy and of liberal government. Much was made in British war propaganda of the fight for 'freedom', and most of the ordinary British people really believed in this. Inevitably this rubbed off on to the politicians, and later the masses, in the subject colonies. Why should Poland or Belgium be liberated, but not them? Churchill, as British wartime prime minister, maintained a robust imperialistic attitude in his words, but his actions, into which events forced him, often belied them. Thus in 1940, the Churchill government pledged that the post-war constitution of India would be settled by an elected constituent assembly. In other words, the principle had been agreed of Indian independence and only questions of timing remained.

Winston Churchill as war-time prime minister maintained an imperialist attitude in his words which his actions often had, of necessity, to belie. In 1942 his government pledged that the post-war constitution of India would be settled by an elected assembly, thus agreeing in principle to Indian independence.

By 1945 the world was dominated by two great powers, the United States and the Soviet Union, neither of which was in sympathy with old-style European colonialism. Thus the British argument that the empire could be justified as a 'civilising mission' received scant international support. Moreover, for internal domestic reasons, the British had elected their first Labour government to have full power, and from the nature of its traditions the Labour Party was out of sympathy with aggressive imperialism. It was the Labour Prime Minister, Clement Attlee, who in 1947 took the final decision on India. The Indian politicians could not decide on their own constitution. The National Congress, dominated by Jawaharlal Nehru, fought until almost the last moment for a united India. The Moslem minority, under Mahomet Ali Jinnah, stood out for a separate Islamic state, Pakistan, for themselves. Attlee simply announced a time limit for British withdrawal, and kept to it. Thus the two new countries were born in conditions of warfare between each other, with deaths that have been computed as running into millions. It followed almost automatically on Indian independence that Burma, Ceylon and Malaya should also become independent, although in the latter case there first had to be a civil war to eliminate largely Communist guerrillas, mainly from China. The Far East was gone.

A disaster of a kind similar to India occurred the following year in Palestine. Under the ambiguous terms of the Balfour Declaration of 1917, the British there were bound to establish a national Jewish 'home'. Under the pressure of the extreme anti-Semitism of the Hitler regime in Germany, the Jews became the more determined to interpret 'home' as 'independent Jewish state' and heavy pressure built up for immigration. The Arab population of Palestine, or many activists among it, resisted the Jewish influx. Extremists on both sides resorted to terrorism. Again, the British decided that the only answer was for them to clear out and again their departure was followed by war. The Jews won to the extent of establishing an independent state of Israel but even decades later no permanent peace had come to the area.

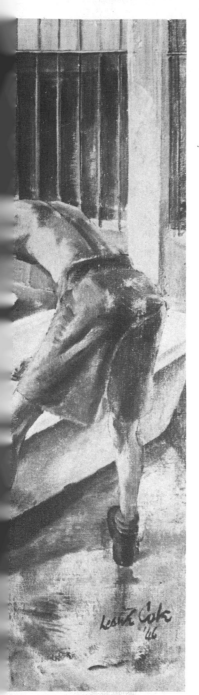

British prisoners of war in Changi Gaol, Singapore, a painting by Leslie Cole. For twenty years the British had been building up Singapore as a naval and military base, with the aim of making it the bastion of British power for the whole of the Far East. In 1942 it fell to the Japanese, a catastrophe which heralded the end of the imperial dream.

Clement Attlee, Labour Prime Minister, who made the final decision on India, announcing, and keeping to, a time limit for British withdrawal.

A side-effect of the Palestine mess was to strengthen nationalism generally among the Arabs of the Middle East. British power among the Arabs, and their oilfields, rested upon a chain of satellite states, nominally independent but really within the British sphere. They included Egypt, Iraq, Jordan and the sheikhdoms of the Persian Gulf. In particular, Egypt with the Suez Canal – 'the lifeline of the Empire' – had long been scarcely more than a British colony. The British maintained in Egypt a garrison of 60,000 men. It was while serving against the Israelis in 1948 that a young Egyptian officer, Gamal Abdel Nasser, formed an ambition to liberate the Middle East from 'the forces and factors that dominate it now'. Nasser, a characteristic, extremist personality, was the mainspring of a revolution which ousted the Egyptian royal dynasty and replaced it with a militantly nationalistic republic. In 1954, Egypt obtained real independence with an agreement by the British to withdraw their forces. Two years later, on Nasser nationalising the Suez Canal, the British, with the French as allies, were back in an attempt to overthrow him by force. The attempt was a fiasco not so much through Egyptian resistance but through world opinion, including the United States and the Soviet Union, being opposed to it. The British and French had to withdraw in diplomatic ignominy and in doing so provided the most practical possible proof that old-style imperialism was no longer viable. Similar nationalist upheavals took place in Iraq and Jordan, and well before the end of the 1950s real British power in the Middle East had vanished. In the island colony of Cyprus the British fought a five-year civil war against the local Greek nationalists, and this, too, ended in British withdrawal and the release of the Cypriot leader.

Africa

But it did seem, even after the Second World War, that the British Empire in Africa would be a long-lasting institution. The bulk of it had been acquired well within living memory, but it seemed to have a quality of permanence. The 1945 Labour Government, for all its relinquishments of power in the Middle and Far East, set about actively developing the African colonies and training new administrative services for them. The underlying assumption was that the empire would continue in Africa at the very least until the end of the century.

Again, though, the Second World War had accelerated things. The first breakthrough came through ex-servicemen in the Gold Coast [now Ghana]. Some 30,000 men from the Gold Coast had served with the British forces in the war. This meant they had travelled beyond their own country, seen something of the world and learned that they had been fighting for 'democracy'. On their return home, they were no longer willing to accept colonialist paternalism. In Kwame Nkrumah, a journalist who had been educated in Britain and the United States, they had a leader of force and ambition. The British briefly tried a policy of repression but then switched to conciliation in the form of what in African terms was a revolutionary new type of constitution, which handed over most of the internal administration to an elected government and parliament. Nkrumah was in prison during the first election under the new constitution; he came straight out of his cell to be chief of the government. The logical next step was independence (internal self-government could never, by its nature, be more than an intermediate stage) and this came in 1956.

What had been granted to the Gold Coast could not be withheld from the other African colonies. The process was speeded up by the Mau Mau rebellion in Kenya and by rather more peaceful types of agitation everywhere else. In the early 1950s the British were still supporting white settlement in the Rhodesias and hoping to form a new Central African Federation as a traditional-type dominion. But by the end of the decade it was a Conservative Prime Minister, Harold Macmillan, who made his 'wind of change' speech at Capetown; this signalled the end of the imperial concept. All that remained was a tidying-up operation in which the former colonies were set up as independent states.

The Commonwealth

Tied in with this final phase was an attempt to keep alive a form of unity in the Commonwealth. The phrase 'British Commonwealth of Nations' had been coined by the South African J. C. Smuts in the First World War. It was supposed to be an association of like-minded countries bound together by ties of kinship and common recognition of the British crown. For a time it had seemed to work well. Britain, Canada, South Africa, Australia and New Zealand had closely similar methods of government, a common language and some identity of interests. But the operation of the 'old Commonwealth' was more a matter of sentiment than of real politics. Even on economic matters there could be little co-operation beyond what would have been dictated by the terms of trade in any case. In 1932, under the Ottawa agreements, the member countries accorded each other a degree of tariff preference. But the fundamental imbalance remained that whereas Britain wanted to use the dominions as a source of raw materials and a market for British manufactured goods, the dominions wanted to have their own manufacturing industries. For such occasions as the 1937 coronation of George VI the dominions proudly associated themselves with Britain. But the business meetings between the wars—the consultations between the prime ministers of the member countries—grew steadily less frequent. South Africa, in any event, was never really happy within the 'family' and the Boer majority in her white population was moving towards the declaration of a republic.

The independence of India and Pakistan brought a basic problem for the Commonwealth. These countries had no blood tie with Britain, intended to become republics, and would certainly pursue independent, even 'neutralist' foreign policies. To accommodate them, Britain gave the monarch the new title of 'Head of the Commonwealth', which had no precise legal meaning, and abolished the conception of common imperial citizenship. Meetings of Commonwealth leaders continued but, as more and more countries became independent, they took on the air of ordinary international conferences rather than of intimate 'family' meetings. The 'new Commonwealth' cannot be compared with the old as a definite force in the world.

In the new world, it became the fashion of the major powers to court the favours of small ones by treating them as important entities and giving them aid. Even the smallest country, which in the nineteenth century would have been incapable of standing on its own in contact with modern powers, could now have its seat at the United Nations and thus a definite international status. With the dissolution of the British and French empires, the membership of the United Nations rose to 122, and even so small a community as the former British colony of the Maldives in the Indian Ocean, only 87,000 strong, was allowed full status. The British Empire left behind it two major problems—the strife between India and Pakistan, and sporadic, prolonged warfare between Israel and the Arab states in the Middle East. The export of Westminster-style government to Africa and Asia was an almost total failure. However, for all its faults, the British Empire did contain a thread of genuine idealism and progress. Although the vague new 'Commonwealth', which has replaced it, has little practical political meaning, it does embody a measure of goodwill which a former colonising power is fortunate to have earned.

Gamal Abdel Nasser, mainspring of the revolution which overthrew the Egyptian royal dynasty and replaced it with a nationalist republic.

Left: *Jewish refugees from Nazism arrive in Palestine. The influx of Jewish immigrants was strongly resented by the Arab population, and terrorist activities on both sides persuaded the British that the only course open to them was to withdraw from Palestine.*

Below: *Anglo-French troops in Port Said, 1956. The British attempt to overthrow Nasser, when the latter nationalised the Suez canal, was a fiasco in terms of world opinion—the British and French had to withdraw in complete ignominy, having incurred the displeasure of both the United States and the Soviet Union.*

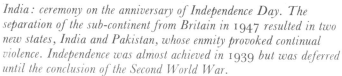

India: ceremony on the anniversary of Independence Day. The separation of the sub-continent from Britain in 1947 resulted in two new states, India and Pakistan, whose enmity provoked continual violence. Independence was almost achieved in 1939 but was deferred until the conclusion of the Second World War.

Celebrations in Ghana before a political meeting. The holiday mood of the crowd was due to the promise that the meeting would be attended by Kwame Nkrumah. Nkrumah, who led his country to independence, was in prison during the first election under the new constitution, but was released in 1951 and became prime minister in 1952.

Left: *Jomo Kenyatta, the revered African leader who endured imprisonment and exile in order to achieve for his country a new constitution and independence from British rule.*

Short reading list

Canada, W. G. Brown, 1950.

The Cambridge History of the British Empire, 1929-63.

The Fall of the British Empire, Colin Cross, 1968.

Imperial Commonwealth, Lord Elton, 1945.

African Survey, Lord Hailey, 1938.

The American People, Oscar Handlin, 1963.

The Colonial Office, Sir Charles Jeffries, 1956.

Facing Mount Kenya, Jomo Kenyatta, 1938, 1961.

A Short History of Central and Southern Africa, S. V. Lumb, 1954.

Pax Britannica, James Morris, 1968.

Britain's Moment in the Middle East, Elizabeth Monroe, 1963.

The Discovery of India, Jawaharlal Nehru, 1946.

The Expansion of Elizabethan England, A. L. Rowse, 1955.

The Story of Australia, A. G. L. Shaw, 1955.

A History of New Zealand, K. Sinclair, 1959.

The Oxford History of India, Vincent A. Smith, edited by Percival Spear, 1958.

Jan Christian Smuts, J. C. Smuts, 1952.

Cross Roads to Israel, Christopher Sykes, 1965.

Botha, Smuts and South Africa, A. F. B. Williams, 1946.

A Short History of British Expansionism, J. A. Williamson, 1958.

Acknowledgments

Colour Plates

18: British Museum (R. B. Fleming & Co). 19 top: Bibliotheque Nationale, Paris. 19 bottom: Marquess of Salisbury, Hatfield House (Hamlyn Group Library). 22–23: National Maritime Museum, London. 23 right: National Portrait Gallery, London. 31 top: British Museum (Hamlyn Group Library). 30–31: Aldrich Rockefeller Folk Art Collection, Williamsburg, Virginia. 39 top: British Museum (B.P.C. Library). 39 bottom: Musée Guimet, Paris. 42 bottom: Victoria & Albert Museum, London (Hamlyn Group Library). 42–43: National Maritime Museum, London. 43 right: Victoria & Albert Museum, London (Hamlyn Group Library). 43 left: Picturepoint Ltd., London. 46: National Army Museum, London. 47 top & bottom: Librairie Hachette, Paris. 66–67: India Office Library, London (R. B. Fleming & Co). 67 right: Victoria & Albert Museum, London (Hamlyn Group Library). 70 left: National Portrait Gallery, London. 71: R. B. Fleming & Co. (Reproduced by courtesy of The Secretary of State for Foreign & Commonwealth Affairs.) 75 top: National Maritime Museum, London. 75 bottom: Royal Geographical Society, London (Hamlyn Group Library). 78–79: National Maritime Museum, London. 79 bottom: National Maritime Museum (Hamlyn Group Library). 98 bottom: National Army Museum, London. 98–99 top: National Maritime Museum, London. 99 bottom: National Army Museum, London. 103 & 107: Daily Telegraph Library. 106–107: National Army Museum, London. 107 bottom: National Army Museum, London. 110: National Portrait Gallery, London. 111 top & Bottom: Royal Geographical Society, London (Hamlyn Group Library). BACK COVER: Imperial War Museum, London (Hamlyn Group Library).

Black & White Illustrations

Half-title: Hamlyn Group Library. Contents page: Radio Times Hulton Picture Library. 6: National Army Museum, London. 7 top: J. Allan Cash; bottom: Horniman Museum, London. 8 top: J. Allan Cash; bottom: Radio Times Hulton Picture Library. 9 top & bottom: Magnum Photos. 10: Culver Pictures Inc., N.Y. 12 top: Hamlyn Group Library; bottom: Giraudon. 12–13: Radio Times Hulton. 14: National Portrait Gallery, London. 15: New York Public Library. 17: Public Archives of Canada. 20: Radio Times Hulton. 21 top: Radio Times Hulton; bottom: Hudson's Bay Company. 24: Radio Times Hulton. 26–27: National Gallery of Canada, Ottawa. 27 top right & bottom: Radio Times Hulton. 28: Librairie Larousse, Paris. 29 top: Hamlyn Group Library; bottom: Beken & Son, Cowes. 32 top: Mansell Collection. 32–33: Culver Pictures Inc., N.Y. 34–35 & 35 top: Radio Times Hulton. 35 bottom: New York Public Library. 36: National Portrait Gallery, London. 38 top: British Museum; bottom: Librairie Hachette, Paris. 40: Mansell Collection.

44–45 top: Royal Geographical Society, London; bottom: Mansell Collection. 49 top: North Carolina Museum of Art; bottom: Mansell Collection. 50–57 Royal Ontario Museum, Toronto. 51 top: New York Public Library; bottom Popperfoto, London. 52–53 top: Radio Times Hulton; bottom: New York Public Library. 53 top right: Methodist Missionary Society; bottom right: Librairie Larousse, Paris. 54 top: New York Public Library; bottom left: Radio Times Hulton. 54–55: Hamlyn Group Library. 57: Radio Times Hulton. 58: American Embassy Library, London. 58–59: Sammlung Handke, Bad Berneck. 60–61: Mansell Collection. 62: Radio Times Hulton. 63: Giraudon. 65, 69: Radio Times Hulton. 72–73 top: Mansell Collection. 72–73, 73 top: Radio Times Hulton. 73 bottom, 74: Hamlyn Group Library. 77 left: British Museum; right: Government Printer, New South Wales; bottom: Dixson Coll. Mitchell Lib., Sydney. 80: Hamlyn Group Library. 81: Victoria & Albert Museum, London. 82: Scala. 84–85: Roger Clark. 85 right: National Army Museum, London. 86: Nan Kivell Coll., National Library of Australia, Canberra. 87: Australian News & Information Bureau, London. 88: Nan Kivell Coll., National Library of Australia, Canberra. 89: Notman Archives, McCord Museum, McGill Univ. Montreal. 90–91: City Archives, Vancouver. 90 bottom, 91 top, 91 bottom: Notman Archives, McCord Museum, McGill Univ. Montreal. 92 top: City Archives, Vancouver. 92 bottom left: Provincial Archives, Victoria, British Columbia. 92 bottom right: Photo Library, New Zealand High Commission, London. 94: Mary Evans Picture Library. 95 top: National Portrait Gallery, London. 95 bottom: Art Gallery, New South Wales. 96: H. Roger Viollet. 100–101: National Army Museum, London. 100 bottom: Radio Times Hulton. 101 top: National Portrait Gallery, London. 101 bottom: Popperfoto, London. 104 left: Radio Times Hulton. 104–105: Hamlyn Group Library. 109 top: India Office Library, London. 109 bottom: Radio Times Hulton. 112: Reproduced by gracious permission of H.M. The Queen. 113: Mansell Collection. 114–115 & 115 left: Popperfoto, London. 115 bottom: National Portrait Gallery, London. 116: South African Archives, Capetown. 118 left: Popperfoto, London. 118 right: Punch. 119: Mansell Collection. 120 top: Radio Times Hulton; bottom: National Army Museum, London. 121: National Archives of Rhodesia, Salisbury. 124–125: Radio Times Hulton. 126 left: Mansell Collection. 126–127 top & bottom: Radio Times Hulton. 129: J. Allan Cash. 131: Hamlyn Group Library. 132–133: Popperfoto, London. 133 top right: Mary Evans Picture Library; bottom right: Radio Times Hulton. 134: India Office Library, London. 136: Radio Times Hulton. 137: Australian News & Information Bureau, London. 138–139 & 139 top right: Popperfoto, London. 139 bottom right: J. Allan Cash. 140: Radio Times Hulton. 141: Deutsche Fotothek, Dresden. 143: Mansell Collection. 144–145, 147 left: Imperial War Museum, London. 147 right: Radio Times Hulton. 148: Camera Press. 149: Hamlyn Group Library. 151 top & bottom; and 152: Camera Press. 153 top: European Picture Service, N.Y. 153 bottom & 154 left: Keystone Press. 154–155 top: Camera Press. 155 bottom: Popperfoto, London.

Index

Numbers in italic refer to captions